To

....

From

....

Date

....

QUIET-TIME
Devotions
FOR WOMEN

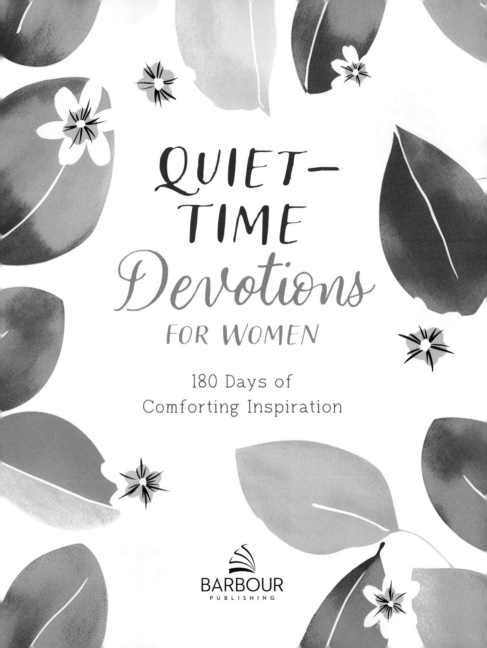

QUIET—TIME

Devotions

FOR WOMEN

180 Days of
Comforting Inspiration

BARBOUR
PUBLISHING

© 2024 by Barbour Publishing, Inc.

Print ISBN 978-1-63609-979-8

All rights reserved. No part of this publication may be reproduced or transmitted for commercial purposes, except for brief quotations in printed reviews, without written permission of the publisher. Reproduced text may not be used on the World Wide Web. No Barbour Publishing content may be used as artificial intelligence training data for machine learning, or in any similar software development.

Churches and other noncommercial interests may reproduce portions of this book without the express written permission of Barbour Publishing, provided that the text does not exceed 500 words or 5 percent of the entire book, whichever is less, and that the text is not material quoted from another publisher. When reproducing text from this book, include the following credit line: "From *Quiet-Time Devotions for Women: 180 Days of Comforting Inspiration*, published by Barbour Publishing, Inc. Used by permission."

Devotions written by: Terry Alburger, Emily Biggers, Jean Fischer, Renee Green, Linda Hang, Anita Higman, Eileen Key, Donna K. Maltese, Kelly McIntosh, Betty Ost-Everley, MariLee Parrish, Carey Scott, Karin Dahl Silver, Rae Simons, Janice Thompson, Stacey Thureen, Annie Tipton, Amy Trent, Ellie Zumbach.

Scripture quotations marked NIV are taken from the HOLY BIBLE, NEW INTERNATIONAL VERSION®. NIV®. Copyright © 1973, 1978, 1984, 2011 by Biblica, Inc.™ Used by permission. All rights reserved worldwide.

Scripture quotations marked NLT are taken from the *Holy Bible*. New Living Translation copyright© 1996, 2004, 2015 by Tyndale House Foundation. Used by permission of Tyndale House Publishers, Inc. Carol Stream, Illinois 60188. All rights reserved.

Scripture quotations marked AMPC are taken from the Amplified® Bible, Classic Edition, Copyright © 1954, 1958, 1962, 1964, 1965, 1987 by The Lockman Foundation. Used by permission.

Scripture quotations marked ESV are from The Holy Bible, English Standard Version®, copyright © 2001 by Crossway Bibles, a publishing ministry of Good News Publishers. The ESV® text has been reproduced in cooperation with and by permission of Good News Publishers. Unauthorized reproduction of this publication is prohibited. All rights reserved.

Scripture quotations marked GW are taken from GOD'S WORD, Copyright © 1995, 2003, 2013, 2014, 2019, 2020 by God's Word to the Nations Mission Society. All rights reserved.

Scripture quotations marked MSG are from *THE MESSAGE*. Copyright © by Eugene H. Peterson 1993, 1994, 1995, 1996, 2000, 2001, 2002. Used by permission of NavPress Publishing Group.

Scripture quotations marked HCSB are taken from the Holman Christian Standard Bible ® Copyright © 1999, 2000, 2002, 2003, 2009 by Holman Bible Publishers. Used by permission.

Scripture quotations marked KJV are taken from the King James Version of the Bible.

Scripture quotations marked NKJV are taken from the New King James Version®. Copyright © 1982 by Thomas Nelson, Inc. Used by permission. All rights reserved.

Published by Barbour Publishing, Inc., 1810 Barbour Drive, Uhrichsville, Ohio 44683, www.barbourbooks.com

Our mission is to inspire the world with the life-changing message of the Bible.

Printed in China.

SPEND SOME QUIET TIME IN THE HEAVENLY FATHER'S PRESENCE TODAY.

Grab your favorite beverage—
coffee, tea, hot cocoa.
Settle into your favorite cozy spot.
Hush your heart.
Then listen for the Lord's voice.

Strengthen your relationship with the heavenly Father as you read through these lovely devotions and prayers designed to help you grow deeper in your faith.

These dozens of practical, inspiring, comforting readings will encourage you to bask in the blessing of personal quiet time with the one who loves you most.

Read on and strengthen your heart-connection to the Master Creator. With each turn of the page, you'll discover a deeper understanding and love for the King of kings and Lord of lords.

Be blessed!

Quiet down before GOD, be prayerful before him.
PSALM 37:7 MSG

SOLITARY PRAYER

Come near to God and he will come near to you.
JAMES 4:8 NIV

Do you have a prayer closet? Jesus said, "And when thou prayest, thou shalt not be as the hypocrites are: for they love to pray standing in the synagogues and in the corners of the streets, that they may be seen of men. Verily I say unto you, they have their reward. But thou, when thou prayest, enter into thy closet, and when thou hast shut thy door, pray to thy Father which is in secret; and thy Father which seeth in secret shall reward thee openly" (Matthew 6:5–6 KJV). So, what did Christ mean by "closet"? The original word is from the Greek *tamion*. It means an inner chamber or secret room.

Jesus warned against people praying in public with the intent to show others how pious they are. Instead, He advocated solitude. Jesus often went off by Himself to draw near to His Father and pray, and that is what He suggested in the passage from Matthew.

A secret room isn't necessary, rather a quiet place where one can be alone with God. Maybe your tamion is your garden or the beach. It might be in the quiet of your own home when your husband and children are away. Wherever it is, enjoy some time alone with God. Draw near to Him in prayer, and He will draw near to you.

Dear God, when we meet in the quiet place,
allow me to breathe in Your presence. Amen.

REST

"Come to me, all you who are weary and
burdened, and I will give you rest."
MATTHEW 11:28 NIV

Only a few weeks into the year, and you are already tired. Somehow, you weren't quite able to shake the problems from last year. And those resolutions you made on day one have already been forgotten. Rest sounds very good right about now, doesn't it?

But the rest that Jesus promises is not a retreat from the world. His rest requires work and education so we can live in the world. We will have to put effort into learning the lessons He has for us. But it will be a shared effort. That's what a yoke is for. It's not meant for just one person to carry on her own. Jesus wants us to be partners with Him in the work. And partners with Him in the rest.

Perhaps that is why God reveals hidden things to little children (see Matthew 11:25). Children tend to carry burdens lightly and drop them easily. They have not yet developed prideful hearts that wish to take on more than they can carry so they can show the world how strong they are. They share their loads as easily as they share secrets or cupcakes.

Are you weary? Are you carrying more than you can support on your own? Come to Jesus. Take on a burden that is only light.

Lord, make my heart gentle and humble like Yours. Amen.

NO PLAYACTOR

*"Be especially careful when you are trying to be good so that you
don't make a performance out of it. It might be good theater, but the
God who made you won't be applauding. When you do something for
someone else, don't call attention to yourself. You've seen them in action,
I'm sure—'playactors' I call them—treating prayer meeting and street
corner alike as a stage, acting compassionate as long as someone is
watching, playing to the crowds. They get applause, true, but that's all
they get. When you help someone out, don't think about how it looks.
Just do it—quietly and unobtrusively. That is the way your God, who
conceived you in love, working behind the scenes, helps you out."*
MATTHEW 6:1–4 MSG

If you were being completely honest with yourself, would you say there
have been times (more often than you'd like to admit) that you've helped
others just for the attention—to get noticed for your good deeds? A
"look what I did" kind of performance? If so, how does it make you feel?

How much better would it feel to do something good for an audience
of one: Jesus? Don't be a "playactor." Rather, work behind the scenes
like Jesus. God will notice your good deeds done quietly and in secret,
and that's what really matters!

*Father God, help me not do things for the recognition I'll get
from others. I want to do good for You and You alone!*

IN THE SILENCE AND STILLNESS

*The Lord was not in the fire; and after the fire
[a sound of gentle stillness and] a still, small voice.
When Elijah heard the voice, he. . .went out.*
1 Kings 19:12–13 AMPC

Right after an amazing demonstration of God's power, during which several of Queen Jezebel's pagan priests were killed, Elijah's life was threatened by the queen herself. Panicked, the prophet ran for his life, traveling "to Beersheba. . .[over eighty miles, and out of Jezebel's realm]" (1 Kings 19:3). Then Elijah traveled even farther, going into the wilderness, where he sat under a tree and asked God to take his life! Instead of killing His prophet, God sent him an angel with food and water. And it was in the strength of that food that Elijah made the forty-day journey to Horeb. There, God passed by him and a huge wind tore apart the mountains. But God wasn't in the wind. Then came an earthquake and a fire, but God wasn't in either.

Elijah finally found God after the fire. For it was then that he heard "[a sound of gentle stillness and] a still, small voice." Hearing that voice, Elijah went out to meet and converse with his Lord.

Need to hear a word from God? Find a place that's quiet. There, in the silence and stillness, you will not only find God but hear His voice.

I come to You, Lord, in the quiet of this moment. Speak, Lord. Speak.

TRUE BEAUTY

Your beauty should not come from outward adornment, such as
elaborate hairstyles and the wearing of gold jewelry or fine clothes.
Rather, it should be that of your inner self, the unfading beauty of
a gentle and quiet spirit, which is of great worth in God's sight.

1 PETER 3:3–4 NIV

Chances are you are inundated by ads for beauty enhancement products and services. Expensive makeup items, hair products, diet aids, clothing, the list goes on and on. The message you get is that beauty is something you can purchase. Yet these material things only enhance your outward appearance. Although they may make you more attractive to yourself or others, Peter reminds you that true beauty cannot be bought but comes from within.

What God values more than anything is your inner self because *that* person is your true being. And having a quiet and gentle spirit is what pleases your Lord.

In Proverbs 31, you can read the description of a woman of noble character. Take particular note of verse 30, which says, "Charm is deceptive, and beauty is fleeting; but a woman who fears the LORD is to be praised." Today and every day, remember that outward beauty is indeed fleeting. But inward beauty never fades, never develops wrinkles, never declines in health. Where does your true beauty lie?

Dear Lord, help me be beautiful on the inside, to focus
my energy on the beauty that matters in Your eyes.

SAY YES!

"Anyone who welcomes you welcomes me, and anyone who welcomes me welcomes the one who sent me. Whoever welcomes a prophet as a prophet will receive a prophet's reward, and whoever welcomes a righteous person as a righteous person will receive a righteous person's reward. And if anyone gives even a cup of cold water to one of these little ones who is my disciple, truly I tell you, that person will certainly not lose their reward."

MATTHEW 10:40–42 NIV

In today's superbusy, run-here-run-there, don't-stop-for-a-minute world, do you ever take the time to pause in the moment and consider the needs of another human being? Or are you stretched so thin that you just can't take a minute to think of anyone other than yourself?

If you find yourself hurried and harried, pause. Right. This. Very. Minute. Quiet your heart. Ask Jesus to calm the chaos in your spirit. Because He *can*. . .and He *will*!

Once your spirit finds the calm it craves, you'll be better able to *really* see the needs of others. Look around! Is there someone who could use your kindness, your hospitality, your generosity? . . . Pinpoint what that person needs—then take action!

In caring for the needs of others, it's as though you're caring for Jesus Himself. Say yes to meeting someone's need today—say yes to Jesus!

Jesus, thank You for helping me recognize the needs of others!

HEALING WORDS

*Pleasant words are as a honeycomb, sweet to
the mind and healing to the body.*
PROVERBS 16:24 AMPC

Ah, sweet words! How they soothe the soul, encourage, and offer hope amid hopelessness. And—the bonus—how they minister to the speaker as well as the hearer.

It's remarkable to think that just a few brief words could change a person's life, but they can. The woman in deep depression? She needs to hear that she's loved. That man who's just lost his job? He needs to hear that he has value and things will get better. That little girl who's feeling lonely and left out? She needs to know that she's loved by you and by God.

It doesn't take long to offer words of hope and healing to those who are in need. And when you see the expression on the recipient's face shift from despair to peace, you'll be so glad you took the time. Perhaps you'll get to watch the sparkle return to that little girl's eyes. Or maybe that woman's despair will lift as you offer words of hope.

Who can you bless today? What words can you speak (whether in person or by text or on social media)? God longs to use you to minister to the very ones who need the most encouragement.

*Show me who I can bless with my words today, Lord.
Ready me in offering a word of love and support. For I
know as I bless, I will be blessed in return. Amen.*

LIVING WATER

"For the Lamb at the center of the throne will be their shepherd; 'he will lead them to springs of living water. And God will wipe away every tear from their eyes.'"

REVELATION 7:17 NIV

The book of Revelation contains a lot of imagery, and the precise meaning of what John saw is debated by many. However, what is *not* debatable are the words of today's verse.

Jesus, the Lamb of God, is at the center of His heavenly throne. He is the shepherd of the survivors of the end days, the ones God deemed worthy. And as their shepherd, Jesus will lead believers to the springs of living water. And God will wipe away their tears and quell their fears.

Are you craving for Jesus to quench your thirst? If so, remember Jesus' words, "Whoever believes in me, as Scripture has said, rivers of living water will flow from within them" (John 7:38). And allow the Lord your shepherd to make you lie down in green meadows and to lead you beside the quiet waters (Psalm 23:1–2). Visualize the abundant water, flowing and calm, and the fact that God will truly wipe every tear from your eyes, bringing you the peace and comfort you're longing for.

Dear Lord, I pray there is a place for me at Your springs of living water. Guide me and console me, that I may live in Your kingdom forever.

SOUL SPEAK

Why are you cast down, O my inner self? And why should you moan over me and be disquieted within me? Hope in God and wait expectantly for Him, for I shall yet praise Him, my Help and my God.

PSALM 42:5 AMPC

Where do you go for help and hope when discouraged? How do you keep your inner self lifted up, expecting good to come?

The author of Psalm 42 spoke to his inner self, his soul, telling it not to be discouraged, sad, or in turmoil. He told himself to hope in God, be patient in waiting for His help, knowing he would praise the God who loves him.

About a thousand years later, both a synagogue leader and an unclean woman expressed the same hope and faith in God as did the psalmist. The religious leader knew that if Jesus laid His hands on his dying daughter, she'd be healed and live (Mark 5:23). The woman who'd been bleeding for twelve years knew Jesus could heal her, and so said to herself with certainty, "If I only touch His garments, I shall be restored to health" (Mark 5:28 AMPC).

No matter what you're going through, hang on to your expectant hope and faith in God. Speak to your soul, knowing His transformational love is being poured out upon you by day, leading you to songs of praise each night (Psalm 42:8).

Pour out Your love upon me today, Lord,
leading me to songs of praise tonight.

BANK ON HIS GENEROSITY

"You may ask, 'What will we eat in the seventh year if we do not plant or harvest our crops?' I will send you such a blessing in the sixth year that the land will yield enough for three years."

LEVITICUS 25:20–21 NIV

Can you imagine regularly taking a year off work and having *no worries* whatsoever? Today's Leviticus reading gives a fascinating look at God's generosity and provision: Every seventh year, the Israelites were to leave the land fallow, a "festival year. . .a year to honor *the LORD*" (25:4 GW). If the Israelites were obedient in this, God promised to provide extra for their needs, far beyond the bare minimum, so they and the land could rest that year.

God's abundance is also seen in Mark, as Jesus feeds the multitude (including five thousand men!) who had followed Him into the countryside to hear Him preach. There were twelve baskets of leftover food *after* the people had eaten "as much as they wanted" (6:42 GW).

Jehovah Jireh, our provider, is delighted to care for His people. What have you been waiting for God to provide? All throughout His Word is evidence of His generosity and compassion. He will provide for your needs for today and for tomorrow—you can bank on it.

Lord, You are a generous God. It's hard to wait for Your answer, but I trust in Your promise that You take care of Your children (see Philippians 4:19).

THE ONE

*What man of you, if he has a hundred sheep and should lose one
of them, does not leave the ninety-nine in the wilderness (desert)
and go after the one that is lost until he finds it? And when he
has found it, he lays it on his [own] shoulders, rejoicing.*

LUKE 15:4–5 AMPC

You may wonder why the shepherd cares so much for just one sheep. After all, he has ninety-nine others for wool or meat. Why should he worry if one goes missing? But the fact of the matter is that the shepherd bought or brought into the world each lamb. He loved and cared for it. The sheep are not just his flock but his companions as he is away from home. Even one means everything to him.

That's how your Lord views you. You were bought with a price and called by name into God's kingdom. Everything changes when you're lost to Him. Everything changes again when you're found by Him.

When you chose to follow Jesus, there was rejoicing in heaven. You. You were the one Jesus died and rose again for. You. You were the one He chases after. You. Rest in and receive that good shepherd's love, that passion He has for you today.

*Dear God, sometimes I forget how much You love me and cherish
me. But today I acknowledge everything You've done in my
life and what You will continue to do in my future. Amen.*

SHIFT GEARS

I will greatly praise the LORD with my mouth;
yea, I will praise him among the multitude.
PSALM 109:30 KJV

Praising God might come naturally to you. Then again, it might not. Yet often it's through praising God that your thoughts become transformed. That's because your focus shifts. Instead of focusing on circumstances or the everyday events, you turn your attention toward your Creator.

Take some time today to praise God and, in turn, transform your thoughts. Here are some ideas:

- Go for a walk and, as you do, notice the beauty of creation. Thank God for all you see, hear, and smell.

- Call, text, or email a friend you haven't talked with for a while. As you catch up, offer to pray for her. If she's a believer, ask her if you can share some of your prayer requests. Then pray for each other.

- Sit quietly in your house, at a nearby coffee shop, or even in your car. Turn off any source of media. Be still, and silently start praising God for the good things that come to the forefront of your mind.

- Listen to worship music. Sing or dance to it.

Lord, show me some unique ways that I can shift gears
and focus on You. As I do, help me praise You in all things.
As I praise You, change and transform my mind.

LETTING GOD FIGHT FOR YOU

The Lord will fight for you, and you shall
hold your peace and remain at rest.
EXODUS 14:14 AMPC

Letting God fight for us can be a tall order because we're capable women, ready and able to handle what comes our way. It may not be pretty, but we get the job done. We are moms and wives, company owners and shift managers, coaches and teachers, and everything in between. And when we're standing in God's strength and wisdom, we're a force to be reckoned with. Amen?

Yet there are times we're to let God fight for us. We're to take a step back and trust as He handles the situation. We're to wait on His timing and plan, even when it seems there's no movement whatsoever. And instead of jumping in and trying to make everything come together, we're to take a seat. We're to let God be God.

What makes that hard for you? Are you more comfortable in the driver's seat? Do you feel better when you're calling the shots? Is it easiest when you get to control all interactions and outcomes?

God is asking you to trust Him enough to surrender your game plan to His. And when you do, you'll find peace.

Lord, I'll admit this is hard for me. I like being in control.
But I know that You are God and I am not. Will You grow
my faith so I can surrender to Your will and way?

SERVE IN TRUST

"For even the Son of Man came not to be served but to serve others and to give his life as a ransom for many."
MARK 10:45 NLT

In today's passage, the disciples were arguing about who would be the greatest among them, entirely missing the true character of God's kingdom. While we may chuckle at their misunderstanding, Jesus' words still have a salient message for us: service is the heart and mark of Christian leadership.

But is there such a thing as "too much" serving? Maybe you genuinely follow Jesus' example in serving others but constantly find yourself spent and worn out, more jaded than joyous. Perhaps you take on too much out of worry, thinking things just "won't get done right" (or at all) if you don't step in. But worries like these may mean you're depending a little too much on yourself. Remember, God is committed to the service you're involved in—even more than you are—and He will make His good work flourish.

We need to exercise our trust muscles to serve well as leaders in our churches, homes, and communities—and that may look like intentionally making time to rest or leaving work (maybe more than we're used to!) to others. Let's follow Jesus' model and stay connected to our source of life, trusting that no matter what, He has it all under control.

Jesus, when it feels like it's all up to me,
remind me You're always at work.

OUR BUMBLY WAYS

They refused to listen and failed to remember the miracles you performed among them. They became stiff-necked and in their rebellion appointed a leader in order to return to their slavery. But you are a forgiving God, gracious and compassionate, slow to anger and abounding in love. Therefore you did not desert them.

NEHEMIAH 9:17 NIV

At times, this life is much like a mountain climb. Some of the trails might be pleasant, while others are rough, foggy, and downright treacherous. Unfortunately, we humans sometimes make the way harder than it is with our rebellion. We might choose a route that we know is deadly, just because it appears enticing. And then that's it—we traipse off on our own without ropes or a compass or our guide. Like sheep gone astray, we find ourselves stumbling into an abyss or a patch of razor-sharp brambles. And then later, bloodied and bone weary, we wonder bitterly what went wrong. We rail at the world, at everyone around us, and even at God.

Throughout history, we've been those bumbly sheep. Thank the Lord—truly—that He is forgiving, gracious, and compassionate, slow to anger and abounding in love. Even in our sheep-like ways, we can rest in those good and lovely truths.

Dearest Lord Jesus, I admit that at times I am one of those bumbly sheep stuck in the brambles. Please keep me on Your path—the one that leads to eternal life. Amen.

HOW SWEET IT IS!

My child, eat honey, for it is good, and the honeycomb is sweet to the taste. In the same way, wisdom is sweet to your soul. If you find it, you will have a bright future, and your hopes will not be cut short.
PROVERBS 24:13–14 NLT

Perhaps you prefer a drizzle of honey to sweeten your hot tea; or maybe you enjoy the flavor of honey on a warm, buttered biscuit. Did you know that in addition to being used as a sweetener, honey is also used for its anti-inflammatory and antibacterial properties? Honey can soothe a sore throat and even help ease the pain of a mild burn.

In the above verses from the book of Proverbs, Solomon is making a connection between honey and wisdom. He observes that both honey and wisdom are sweet and beneficial. Just as honey sweetens whatever it touches, wisdom sweetens your life!

If you have a relationship with God, you're already on the right track to finding wisdom. In addition to spending quality time with Him and reading His Word, all you need to do is ask for wisdom, and He'll provide it for you (James 1:5). "Eat up" every bit of wisdom the heavenly Father provides!

Father, give me the wisdom Solomon writes about in the Proverbs. I long to have a life abundant in unshakable hope. . .and a bright future too! Thank You for keeping the promises in Your Word. Amen.

A QUIET HEART AND A CALM SOUL

God, I'm not trying to rule the roost, I don't want to be king of the mountain. I haven't meddled where I have no business or fantasized grandiose plans. I've kept my feet on the ground, I've cultivated a quiet heart. Like a baby content in its mother's arms, my soul is a baby content.

PSALM 131:1–2 MSG

Oh, if only you had your way, if only people would listen to you, if only you could be queen, you could straighten out this world.

Have you ever felt like that? If so, that's the exact opposite of what God wants you to be feeling. He loves the humble, those who long to surrender to Him and serve others. When you leave all your plans and worries in His hands, He lifts you up (1 Peter 5:6–7; James 4:10), guides you, and teaches you what's right (Psalm 25:9). When you give Him complete control, God transforms your defeat to victory (Psalm 149:4).

Jesus said the kingdom of heaven was made up of people who were like little children (Matthew 19:14). So ask God to help you cultivate a quiet heart. To make you a trusting daughter, one whose soul is calm, just like a baby who finds her contentment in her mother's arms.

Lord, transform my heart and soul. Help me trust You with all things, stay humble, have a quiet heart and a calm soul, content in Your loving arms.

THE RESCUER

"But I will rescue you on that day, declares the Lord;
you will not be given into the hands of those you fear."
JEREMIAH 39:17 NIV

As the voice of God, Jeremiah endured many hardships while living in a land besieged by Babylonians. Thrown into a pit and left to die, Jeremiah was saved by a brave man named Ebed-Melech. God repaid the courage of this man with the promise of protection from those he feared, those who would take him prisoner.

Just as God promised to protect Ebed-Melech, He promised to protect Joshua. In Deuteronomy 3:22, God reminds him, "Do not be afraid of them; the Lord your God himself will fight for you."

Fear is something against which everyone struggles. And there will be many situations in which each of us will have to face our fear. Yet all we need to do is remember God's words telling His people to rest assured, to not be afraid.

The Lord your God *will* rescue you on your hardest days. He *will not* deliver you into the hands of your darkest fears but *will* bring you into the light and protection of His presence.

Dear Lord, the words You gave me through Your Son,
Jesus Christ, tell me that You will deliver me from evil.
I pray You will take away my fears and in my darkest
day will rescue me from the depths of despair.

SETTLED PLANS

Jesus replied, "If I want him to remain alive until I return,
what is that to you? As for you, follow me."

JOHN 21:22 NLT

Jesus questioned Peter about his love. . .then Jesus predicted martyrdom for his future. Peter's total commitment to Jesus would be a *total* commitment. Close on the heels of Jesus' words, Peter looked around, saw John, and asked Jesus, "What about him?" The verses don't give us clues about Peter's tone, whether he was petulant, dismayed, or just curious. But Jesus' response is clear: "Leave that in My hands. Concentrate on following Me."

God's plans for us are not factory produced and one size fits all. They are handmade and carefully tailored. That fact is a delight when His plan is something we would have chosen ourselves. But what if it isn't? What if our hopes and dreams never come true? What if we receive an unwanted diagnosis? What if we start looking around and asking, "But what about them?"

The only way to be steady in God's plans for us individually is to leave the planning in His hands and concentrate on following Him. We trust God with our eternal lives. Can we not trust Him with our earthly lives too?

God, Your plans for me may not be my first choice, but I choose
to rest in Your will. When I begin to wonder why my life isn't
like others', remind me that You never make mistakes.

SOUL CELEBRATIONS

And on that day they offered great sacrifices, rejoicing because God had given them great joy. The women and children also rejoiced. The sound of rejoicing in Jerusalem could be heard far away.
NEHEMIAH 12:43 NIV

Oh, when we get it right with God, ahh yes, our souls can't help but rejoice—just as they did in the days of old. What have your unique times of "soul celebrations" looked like? Did they come as a praise, a shout, or a song? And how did you come by that joy? Was it the day you walked away from a temptation that had previously tangled you in its web? Or was it in the moment when you genuinely cheered for a friend's engagement even though that dream of marriage has always eluded you? Perhaps it was when you went back to the store to pay for an item that had accidentally gotten left off your bill. Or could it be the deliberate pause amid a harried life to take in the wonder of God's creation?

The world may not delight in these kinds of life happenings, but the Lord does. May we ever rejoice in what is good and right and lovely in the sight of God. May we all fall into step with the Lord, bring Him delight, and know joy everlasting.

Lord, may my life delight You and my soul celebrations bring attention to Your majesty and mercy. In Jesus' name I pray. Amen.

28

KEY TO HAPPINESS

He will be the sure foundation for your times,
a rich store of salvation and wisdom and knowledge;
the fear of the LORD is the key to this treasure.
ISAIAH 33:6 NIV

During the days of Isaiah, things were downright scary in Jerusalem. The Assyrian army was ravaging everything in sight, threatening Jerusalem's very existence. But Isaiah was the voice of calm, revealing God's words to His people, assuring them that God would save them.

The words of Isaiah resonated with the people then as they do now. The key, as Isaiah tells us, is to fear the Lord. In this case, the word *fear* does not mean to be afraid but rather to have respect and reverence. This is the same way we "fear" our parents or those in authority.

What is "this treasure" of which Isaiah speaks? Unlike a chest overflowing with gold and jewels, Isaiah refers to a treasure far more valuable. This treasure offers safety, peace of mind, knowledge, and wisdom. As Proverbs 8:11 tells us, "Wisdom is more precious than rubies, and nothing you desire can compare with her."

Remember to let God be your foundation, and you will certainly reap the bounty of His treasure.

Dear Lord, help me to trust in You, to respect You, and to be secure in the knowledge that my confidence lies in You. Help me seek the treasure You offer, the true treasure of salvation, wisdom, and knowledge.

INHERITING HONOR

He mocks proud mockers but shows favor to the humble and
oppressed. The wise inherit honor, but fools get only shame.

PROVERBS 3:34–35 NIV

How many times do you see commercials showing poor people sliding behind the wheel of a luxury vehicle? Or how often do you see oppressed people walking down red carpets and receiving awards in glamorous ceremonies?

While the world has its own set of standards about what makes a person rich, admirable, successful, or worthy of honor, God's standards are pretty simple. The people He honors are those who do two things— love Him and love others.

In God's kingdom, those who're humble are highly favored. Those who're pushed down by the world are lifted up in His hands. If we want to be among those inheriting honor from God, we have to be wise in His sight. We have to listen to Him and follow Him. We have to be people who are generous and open with our neighbors—people who trust God and are trustworthy. People who choose peace over violence, care over conflict, and love above all.

No doubt there will be some who mock us for the way we choose to live our lives. There will be many who don't understand. But perhaps when they see the blessings of God we receive—the peace and quiet, happy confidence that comes through living for Him—they will stop their mocking and be drawn to Him too.

Lord, keep me humble. Amen.

THE ENEMY'S TACTICS

One day he went into the house to attend to his duties. . . .
She caught him by his cloak and said, "Come to bed with
me!" But he left his cloak in her hand and ran.

GENESIS 39:11–12 NIV

The enemy is sly! He comes after you in such tricky ways that you don't always recognize his tactics. That's why it's so important to keep your guard up!

Maybe you've been there. You were trekking along just fine. Then, from out of the blue, you were hit with a false accusation or relationship struggle. You spent the first few minutes reeling, because it didn't make sense. Then, as the dust cleared, you began to see it for what it truly was. . .an attack.

When the enemy comes after you, you can (a) turn and run or (b) look him in the face and call him on his game. But remember, "No weapon forged against you will prevail, and you will refute every tongue that accuses you" (Isaiah 54:17 NIV).

The enemy can try all he likes, but you're God's anointed and covered by Him. Best of all, He'll fight your battles for you. So, don't panic when false accusations come. Don't let the attacks shake you or bring you down. God's going to rush to your defense. All you need to do is quiet your heart and trust Him.

I trust You, Lord, even when everything inside of me is
shaking in anger. I'll look to You, my defender! Amen.

TAKE A TIME – OUT

And they went and woke him, saying, "Save us, Lord;
we are perishing." And he said to them, "Why are you
afraid, O you of little faith?" Then he rose and rebuked
the winds and the sea, and there was a great calm.

MATTHEW 8:25–26 ESV

During Jesus' ministry, He healed many people and performed miracles. Yet today's readings make it clear that putting faith, hope, and trust in Jesus most likely won't make life any easier. But having a relationship with Him can help provide healing, peace, inspiration, wisdom, and direction in an often chaotic and callous world.

The disciples sitting in the boat with Jesus had calamity all around them. A storm had surged at sea, and they were anxious about what to do. Like children who awaken their parents during a middle-of-the-night thunderstorm, the disciples woke up Jesus because they believed He had the authority and power to calm the water. And they were right. When Jesus rebuked the winds and the sea, those elements of nature obeyed. Like misbehaving children on the verge of receiving a time-out, the winds and waves ceased.

Take some time out today to be with God. Share with Him the areas in your life that need healing and peace. Then follow His guidance, assured He *will* calm your storms within and without.

Lord, help me carve time out of my day to be
with You. I long for Your miraculous touch.

JUST A FEW

A truly wise person uses few words.
PROVERBS 17:27 NLT

Women talk more than men: fact or fiction?

Despite your own opinion about this statement, researchers are divided on whether it's true and whether there's a biological reason one way or the other. Regardless of whether we're the chatty sort or generally quiet, scripture is clear: to be wise, talk less.

So why are few words better than a whole slew? Consider:

1. It's impossible to listen while talking. "Understand this, my dear brothers and sisters: You must all be quick to listen, slow to speak, and slow to get angry." James 1:19 NLT

2. Truly listening results in more thoughtful replies. "There is more hope for a fool than for someone who speaks without thinking." Proverbs 29:20 NLT

3. Speaking fewer words can give each one more importance, and you'll likely choose them more carefully. "Let everything you say be good and helpful, so that your words will be an encouragement to those who hear them." Ephesians 4:29 NLT

You know the difference between idle chatter and meaningful conversation. When you hear yourself talking just for talking's sake, take a breath and listen. Without the noise of your own voice, you may just hear God speak in a new and active way!

God, teach me the discipline of listening and thinking before I speak.
Give me the right words that are filled with Your truth. Amen.

EVERLASTING PEACE

Peace I leave with you; My [own] peace I now give and bequeath to you. Not as the world gives do I give to you. Do not let your hearts be troubled, neither let them be afraid. [Stop allowing yourselves to be agitated and disturbed; and do not permit yourselves to be fearful and intimidated and cowardly and unsettled.]

JOHN 14:27 AMPC

Do you want to be free of worry and fear? Want to live a life filled with peace and calm? Jesus holds the answer!

Yes, Jesus has left His peace with you. And this peace, *His* peace, is not the kind of peace the world holds. His is a supernatural peace. And it is found in the presence and strength of God and His Word. *But,* you may be asking, *How can this be? How can I access this amazing and unsurpassed peace Jesus talks about?* By calling on the comforter, aka "the Counselor, Helper, Intercessor, Advocate, Strengthener, Standby" (John 14:26). You know, the Holy Spirit, the one God sent down in Jesus' name to teach you and remind you of things Jesus has already told you in His Word (John 14:26).

Today, stop allowing yourself to be frightened and freaked out. Instead, seek God's presence and receive His peace.

Here I am, Lord, before You. Bless me,
pour upon me, Your everlasting peace.

ALL YOUR LOVE

"Listen, O Israel! The Lord is our God, the Lord alone.
And you must love the Lord your God with all your
heart, all your soul, and all your strength."

<small>DEUTERONOMY 6:4–5 NLT</small>

Jesus called today's verse the "greatest commandment" (Matthew 22:38). It's also the hardest, as it asks for the totality of our love. While we show our love for God by following His Word (see Deuteronomy 6:1–2), we learn to love Him by meditating on His beauty and character.

So let's love the one whose power rescued a nation from four hundred years of oppression, through mighty wonders bringing her out safely to a good land (see Deuteronomy 6:20–25). Let's adore the Creator whose words wrought the earth, whose command silences the angry winds and seas. Let's bow in reverence before the God who drew near to His creation to restore it, who "gave himself for us to redeem us. . .to purify for himself a people that are his very own" (Titus 2:14 NIV). Let's sing of His daily provision, His food for the hungry, His comfort to the hurt and lonely, His mercies that are new every morning.

Hear, O daughter! The Lord is your God, the Lord alone! His salvation is greater than any gift you could bring Him. . .and yet it's your love, your heart, that He desires.

Father, I'll walk in obedience, secure in
Your love for me, responding in trust.

WHEN YOU CAN'T PRAY

And the Holy Spirit helps us in our weakness. For example,
we don't know what God wants us to pray for. But the Holy Spirit
prays for us with groanings that cannot be expressed in words.
And the Father who knows all hearts knows what the Spirit is saying,
for the Spirit pleads for us believers in harmony with God's own will.
ROMANS 8:26–27 NLT

Sometimes we literally cannot pray. The Holy Spirit takes over on such occasions. Go before God; enter into His presence in a quiet spot where there will not be interruptions. And just be still before the Lord. When your heart is broken, the Holy Spirit will intercede for you. When you have lost someone or something precious, the Holy Spirit will go before the Father on your behalf. When you are weak, the comforter will ask the Father to strengthen you. When you are confused and anxious about a decision that looms before you, the counselor will seek God's best for you. You are not alone. You are a precious daughter of the living God. And when Christ ascended into heaven, He did not leave you on this earth to forge through the wilderness on your own. He sent a comforter, a counselor, the Holy Ghost, the Spirit of truth. When you don't know what to pray, the Bible promises that the Spirit has you covered.

Father, please hear the groaning of the Holy Spirit who
intercedes on my behalf before Your throne. Amen.

ON STANDBY

There stood by my side an angel of the God to Whom I belong and Whom I serve and worship, and he said, Do not be frightened, Paul! It is necessary for you to stand before Caesar; and behold, God has given you all those who are sailing with you.

ACTS 27:23–24 AMPC

Paul was handed over with some other prisoners and put on a ship to Italy, but inclement weather threw the ship into dire straits. As the storm kept raging, the hungry men began to lose all hope. That's when Paul stood up and restored it.

Paul told the men an angel had stood by him and told him to not be frightened. (Just like the Lord had stood by Paul and told him to take courage [Acts 23:11].) He told Paul that God's plans would not be thwarted and that God would not just protect Paul but all the men with him.

Because Paul had given himself completely to God, he could speak and act with calm assurance. He could then pass this God-given confidence to his companions, telling them, "Keep up your courage, men, for I have faith (complete confidence) in God that it will be exactly as it was told me" (Acts 27:25).

Live your life with calm assurance knowing the Lord and His angels are on standby, ready to come when you call.

Lord, thank You for being with me on every stage of my voyage.

PATIENT ENDURANCE

Patient endurance is what you need now, so that you will continue to do God's will. Then you will receive all that he has promised.
HEBREWS 10:36 NLT

Patience is a word often associated with waiting—in a line, in a reception area, for a special day on the calendar, for a loved one's arrival. And when a mom instructs a child to be patient, she's probably asking her to be still and quiet while she waits.

Endurance is a word often used to describe what it takes to be a long-distance runner. It connotes grueling, unrelenting work toward a goal, coupled with a runner's confidence of completing that goal and the hope of a race well run.

Hebrews 10:36 urges us believers to practice *patient endurance* as we do God's will then wait to receive all that God has promised. To do so quietly while unrelentingly working toward our goal. We can do that by expecting God to move according to His timing. To anticipate receiving all He has promised as we do His will. That means to get busy, to endure, and endeavor to do God's work where we are, with the unique abilities and passions with which He's gifted us, using them to love God and others (Mark 12:30–31).

Father, I admit I struggle with patience. My head knows Your timing is perfect, but my selfish heart wants everything You've promised NOW. Give me good work to do as I strive toward the goal. Amen.

FINDING YOUR WAY

Whether you turn to the right or to the left, your ears will hear
a voice behind you, saying, "This is the way; walk in it."
ISAIAH 30:21 NIV

Have you ever felt lost, not knowing which way to turn? You stand there, undecided, not sure if you should turn to the left or right. If left to your own devices, you could easily make the wrong choice. In times of weakness, you might react with emotion rather than with faith. You might feel alone, incapable of making a good decision.

Woman of the Way, remember that you are *never* truly alone. God is always there for you, always directing you, whispering in your ear, nudging you to go right or left. Because He has promised never to leave you, you can be assured He is in your corner, behind you, gently ushering you along the path He's laid out for you.

When you find yourself at the crossroad, unsure which way to turn, pray for God's divine directions. Then listen quietly, assured that He'll never abandon you, that He knows what you need, that He has you in His sights and watches over you day and night.

Little lamb, look to your shepherd. And He will guide you safely home.

Dear God, help me to be still, to listen for Your direction,
and to follow wherever You lead. I look to You, my shepherd,
to be the voice behind me, telling me which way to go.

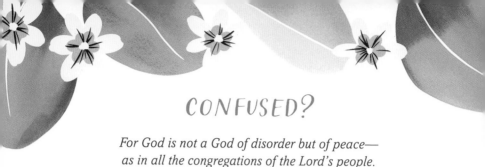

CONFUSED?

For God is not a God of disorder but of peace—
as in all the congregations of the Lord's people.

1 CORINTHIANS 14:33 NIV

"God is not a God of disorder." Yet there is so much dissension within different religious denominations, even within churches. One would think that groups that worship together based on the same teachings would be in harmony. But then one would be wrong.

Your God is a god of peace. God does not encourage disorder, dissension, or confusion. Instead, He promotes peace. Jesus too was a person of peace. Like Father, like Son.

Today's verse encourages you to take God's path, to seek peaceful solutions. When faced with a difficult situation, consider asking yourself, "WWJD. What would Jesus do?" More than a catchy slogan emblazoned on bracelets or T-shirts, WWJD is a reminder to all believers that Jesus, whom they are to emulate, almost always opted for the peaceful path. And just as Jesus was led by His Father in all His actions, so will God lead you in all His actions, including in the ways of peace.

Remember, peace, complete tranquility and serenity, has been promised to believers. And it's that peace, "the peace of God, which transcends all understanding" that "will guard your hearts and your minds in Christ Jesus" (Philippians 4:7).

Dear Lord, please make me an instrument of Your peace.
Help me to be a calming voice of reason in disorder
and to encourage Your peace to all I encounter.

BEAUTIFUL LILIES

*"That is why I tell you not to worry about everyday life—whether you
have enough food and drink, or enough clothes to wear. Isn't life more
than food, and your body more than clothing? Look at the birds. They
don't plant or harvest or store food in barns, for your heavenly Father
feeds them. And aren't you far more valuable to him than they are?
Can all your worries add a single moment to your life? And why worry
about your clothing? Look at the lilies of the field and how they grow.
They don't work or make their clothing, yet Solomon in all his glory was
not dressed as beautifully as they are. And if God cares so wonderfully
for wildflowers that are here today and thrown into the fire tomorrow,
he will certainly care for you. Why do you have so little faith?"*

MATTHEW 6:25–30 NLT

Do you often worry about everyday things in life—like food and
clothing? Or do you instead leave all your worries in the hands of your
perfectly capable provider, your heavenly Father?

If you're a worrywart, these verses from the Gospel of Matthew
should set your mind to rest and lead you to a place of tranquil
transformation. . .from worry to wonder! For the God who cares for the
birds and wildflowers also cares for you!

*Heavenly Father, I trust You—the caretaker of all
creation. . .the birds, the beautiful lilies, and me!*

FROM SICKBED TO SERVANT'S HEART

And when Jesus entered Peter's house, he saw his
mother-in-law lying sick with a fever. He touched her hand,
and the fever left her, and she rose and began to serve him.

MATTHEW 8:14–15 ESV

Peter's mother-in-law was terribly ill on the day that Jesus came by for a visit. If you've ever been down for the count with the flu or other feverish bug, you can imagine how she was feeling—definitely not up to a houseguest.

Oh, but this guest was different from all the others. He walked in, reached to touch her hand, and the fever immediately left her. (Can you imagine?) She jumped up out of bed and did what any hostess would do—began to serve Him.

Maybe you've been through a season of illness or pain and have wished Jesus would sweep in and touch you like that. You've prayed for instantaneous healing, but it didn't come in such a sweeping, awe-inspiring way.

Don't give up. Don't let the wait shake your faith. Just remember that one gentle touch from the Savior was enough to change absolutely everything. Keep your focus on Him until that moment comes.

I won't give up, Lord. I'm ready to rise from this sickbed
and do great things for You. Touch me, I pray. Amen.

BLESSED TO BE A BLESSING

And the Lord said to Moses, Say to Aaron and his sons, This is the way you shall bless the Israelites. Say to them, The Lord bless you and watch, guard, and keep you; The Lord make His face to shine upon and enlighten you and be gracious (kind, merciful, and giving favor) to you; The Lord lift up His [approving] countenance upon you and give you peace (tranquility of heart and life continually). And they shall put My name upon the Israelites, and I will bless them.
NUMBERS 6:22–27 AMPC

This priestly blessing is often recited as a benediction, a prayer used to bless others.

In Numbers, this special prayer comes right after the instructions the Lord gave Moses for purity in Israel's camp, protecting marital faithfulness, and Nazarite laws. Like many of the commands that Moses receives from the Lord, those followed through on brought blessings upon God's people.

While you don't need to perform the tasks that God gave to Moses, He does care about your heart and mind the same way He cared for those of His people long ago. God cares about your physical body and spiritual soul too. Your job is to remain obedient to His leading and purpose for service.

Jesus, keep my mind fixed and focused on You at all times so I may be a blessing to others. In return, show me just how blessed I am to be Your daughter.

UPSIDE DOWN OR DOWNSIDE UP?

" 'You must keep the Israelites separate from things that make
them unclean, so they will not die in their uncleanness for
defiling my dwelling place, which is among them.' "
LEVITICUS 15:31 NIV

Today, it might be challenging to find the good in reading about cleansing from defiling molds and discharges that cause uncleanliness. You might think it a very upside-down approach to your daily faith walk. But, let's turn it downside up for a moment.

This topsy-turvy text has a bottom line. A big idea that God wants His daughters to be aware of. The more you entertain sin and feed temptation, the more they grow and become moldy. The more you allow yourself to live in denial of your habits, the more you become unclean. This creates separation between you and God. In turn, your ability to witness to others weakens. *And* your less-than-desirable actions shed a bad light on the church and body of believers in your community of faith.

By continuing to do what you are already doing—reading God's Word daily, praying, meditating on scripture, seeking Him more than earthly things—the more your mind will become in step with the Holy Spirit's gentle conviction and promptings.

Holy Spirit, I invite You to fill my mind and body with Your
goodness and will for my life. Show me the things I need to clean
up and declutter so I can be pure before You and others.

STEP BACK, STAND STILL

"Now then, stand still and see this great thing
the LORD is about to do before your eyes!"
1 SAMUEL 12:16 NIV

A million potential solutions are ricocheting around in your mind. You finally pick one, then another, but both fall short of the need. You're biting your lip, chewing your nails, then take action once again, doing all you feel you can in the circumstances. But still things aren't exactly right, it seems. Here's where you might want to ask yourself a few questions. Have you talked to God? Have you brought Him into the situation, told Him all the particulars? Have you given Him any room at all in which to work? Or have you only done so up to a certain point and then given up? Perhaps you've determined that you *do* have the answer after all and are taking the proverbial bull by the horns once more?

There are times when God asks you to do some things, when He needs your hands, feet, and mind in a situation. But there are also times when He wants you to just stand back and be still. Give Him time and space. Trust and rest in Him. And then watch and see the fantastic thing He's about to do—right before your eyes! In other words, don't just do something—stand there!

Lord, I don't know what to do, but I know You do.
Help me step back, stand still, and watch You work.

ALONE TIME

*Very early in the morning, while it was still dark,
Jesus got up, left the house and went off to a
solitary place, where he prayed.*

MARK 1:35 NIV

When reading the Gospels, we can learn a lot from paying close attention to Jesus' actions. This short verse tells us that Jesus knew how important it is to find time to be alone with God. We might think that since He is the Son of God, He wouldn't need to seek out quiet prayer times when He walked the earth, since He carried God with Him everywhere He went. But Jesus was also human, and He knew that the busier we are, the more we need to make time for prayer and solitude. Otherwise, life's busyness can take all our attention, making it harder for us to sense God's presence.

During the final three years of Jesus' life, He was constantly busy, with crowds of people following Him everywhere He went—and still, He valued His prayer time so much that He was willing to get up early and find somewhere to be alone. He knew our busy days go better when they start with prayer.

*Remind me, Jesus, that the busier and more active my
life is, the more I need to find alone time with You.*

EVERYTHING WILL BE FINE

"Get going. . . . I will send an angel before
you. . . . I will personally go with you."
EXODUS 33:1–2, 14 NLT

God wanted Moses to lead His people to a new place, a land flowing with milk and honey. Yet that new place was one the Egyptian-born Moses had never seen! And he was not to just *go* there himself but to lead God's people there!

Moses knew he was special to God, so he earnestly prayed, "If it is true that you look favorably on me, let me know your ways so I may understand you more fully and continue to enjoy your favor" (Exodus 33:13 NLT). God replied, "I will personally go with you, Moses, and I will give you rest—everything will be fine for you" (Exodus 33:14 NLT).

When God calls you down a new path, know He'll be with you. Instead of focusing on the what-ifs, stressing about the details, trust God's plan for you.

Remember that because God favors you, His angel has already arrived in the place you're bound. So relax. God promises, "Everything will be fine for you" because you walk with Him. And God keeps His promises, just as He "keeps" you.

I'm not very fond of change, Lord. But I know You want me
to head down a different road. So Lord, help me understand
You more so I can rest easy as we walk together.

PATIENT ENDURANCE

*May the Lord lead your hearts into a full understanding
and expression of the love of God and the patient
endurance that comes from Christ.*

2 THESSALONIANS 3:5 NLT

Notice that this verse speaks of hearts, understanding, and expression, linking our emotions, our mind, and our actions into one unified spiritual journey whose destination is the love of God. Paul, who wrote this letter to the church at Thessalonica, knew from personal experience that the spiritual pathway is filled with both joy and challenges.

We live in a culture that values speed and looks for instant gratification, but when Paul spoke of "patient endurance," he was talking about a willingness to wait, a commitment to keep going even when our progress is so slow it hardly seems we're going anywhere at all. This is a perspective that measures success not by showy achievements but rather by a quiet determination that's rooted deeply in our relationship with Christ.

*Jesus, teach me Your patience, Your willingness to endure
pain and loneliness and misunderstanding. May I come
to understand Your love more and more—and may my
life express Your love to everyone I encounter.*

DAILY BREAD

"Two things I ask of you, Lord. . . . Keep falsehood and lies
far from me; give me neither poverty nor riches, but give me
only my daily bread. Otherwise, I may have too much and
disown you and say, 'Who is the Lord?' Or I may become
poor and steal, and so dishonor the name of my God."

PROVERBS 30:7–9 NIV

Daily bread. It's that which is enough for today and today alone, without worrying about that which is needed in order to sustain you tomorrow.

Jesus, who was also God, came into this world as an infant, humbly, quietly, unnoticed by most. He'd no bed for a crib, was laid in a feeding trough for animals. He relied upon His heavenly Father to sustain Him.

Daily bread keeps us dependent on our Father. For it's just what we need, nothing less and nothing more. He gives us bread for each day. Were we to hoard away more, we might forget our utter dependence on Him and think that we could rely upon our careful plans and resources, upon ourselves.

God rebuked the Israelites for attempting to save up manna rather than accepting it each new day from His hand. Trust in your Father to nourish you in every way, day by day. Thank Him tonight for your daily bread.

God, thank You for providing for me day by day. May I
learn to trust in You far more than I trust in myself.

GOD'S PRESENCE

I pray You, if I have found favor in Your sight, show me now Your way, that I may know You [progressively become more deeply and intimately acquainted with You, perceiving and recognizing and understanding more strongly and clearly] and that I may find favor in Your sight. . . . And the Lord said, My presence shall go with you, and I will give you rest. . .for you have found favor, loving-kindness, and mercy in My sight and I know you personally and by name.

EXODUS 33:13–14, 17 AMPC

Yet again, the Bible indicates to us that external circumstances are interwoven with both our spiritual and emotional lives. As we learn to experience God internally, we will begin to see His presence more clearly in what's going on around us. And as we experience God's activity in the external world, we will also come to know Him more intimately at the spiritual and emotional levels. God is present in it all—and He knows us each by name.

Loving Lord, teach me to recognize Your ways in the world around me. Fill my inner being with the knowledge of Your presence. Help me to rest in You.

STIRRING UP ANGER

"For as churning cream produces butter, and as twisting the nose produces blood, so stirring up anger produces strife."
<small>PROVERBS 30:33 NIV</small>

Have you ever been guilty of stirring up trouble? We all know deep down when we are doing it, but something in us (called a sin nature) tells us to carry on. It can seem a small offense at the time. After all, what's a little gossip shared in the office? What is the big deal about teasing? Can't your spouse take a joke? And so you were a little tough on the kids. . .they still don't have the right to lose their cool just because they felt agitated with you. Right? Or perhaps, if we are honest, we know it is *not so right.*

The Bible warns us about stirring up anger. In Proverbs we read that it creates strife. Do you really want to live with conflict and friction in your relationships? Like many things, this can result in a snowball effect. What starts out as a "joke" or harmless "tidbit of knowledge" can cause a bit of discord, which then may bring about major division.

Take God's Word at face value. Stay far away from things like rumor spreading and sarcasm. Instead, be found as one with a gentle and quiet spirit that's pleasing to the Lord.

Lord, set a guard over my lips. I want to be a peacemaker not a peace breaker.

MIDNIGHT CONFESSION

After he had taken the census, David's conscience began to bother him. And he said to the LORD, "I have sinned greatly by taking this census. Please forgive my guilt, LORD, for doing this foolish thing." The next morning the word of the LORD came.

2 SAMUEL 24:10–11 NLT

Things had been going well for David. . .until one day he was prompted to count all the soldiers in the kingdom. Some say such a census showed David was not trusting in the Lord but in the strength and number of his mighty men. Whatever the case may be, afterward David felt guilty. For some reason, his actions did not sit right with him. His guilty conscience disrupting his sleep, he finally turned to God, asking forgiveness for what his foolishness had prompted him to do. The morning following his midnight confession, the prophet Gad came and relayed the Lord's message to David.

Sometimes, when prompted by God only knows what, we, without thinking, do something foolish. A guilty conscious and sleepless nights may follow—and will most likely continue unless we, like David, talk to God, tell Him what we've done, and ask forgiveness for being such fools. When this is done, what will most likely follow is an overwhelming sense of relief, and then a message from or a mind-merge with the Lord—and a good night's rest.

How have you been sleeping lately?

Something is bothering me, Lord. Can we talk?

OPEN EYES

You're a fountain of cascading light, and you open our eyes to light.
Keep on loving your friends; do your work in welcoming hearts.
PSALM 36:9–10 MSG

Every once in a while, a situation comes up in which we see our true colors, who we really are. At such times, we may not like what we see. That's what happened to Peter, the disciple who told Jesus he'd never desert Him (Matthew 26:33). But Jesus—who knows all and sees all—knew better. He knew that after He was arrested, Peter would deny being with Jesus or even knowing Him. And Peter did, in fact, deny Jesus—not once but three times! The third time, Jesus' words came back to Peter: "Before the rooster crows, you will deny me three times" (Matthew 26:75 MSG). That's when Peter, full of realization and regret, faced with who he truly was, went out and cried.

Yet later, after this scene and several more, Jesus rose again, had breakfast with His followers, and gave Peter another chance (John 21:15–17). He instructed Peter to tend His sheep. A task that Peter took up immediately, never losing his faith in or denying Jesus ever again.

As you continue your transformational journey with Jesus, there may be times you'll trip up and discover you're not who you thought you were. Yet Jesus will never leave you. He'll find you once more, continue to love you, and work in your heart.

Thank You, Jesus, for continuing to love me, no matter what.

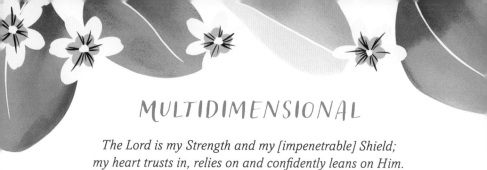

MULTIDIMENSIONAL

The Lord is my Strength and my [impenetrable] Shield;
my heart trusts in, relies on and confidently leans on Him.
PSALM 28:7 AMPC

Who is God to you?

David, the singer and writer of Psalm 28, calls God his rock. He asks Him to listen to his prayer and pleas. He voices and outlines his troubles, concerns, and fears. And before God does anything in his situation, David blesses Him, just for listening to his prayer.

God was not just David's strength—He was his shield. A shield that no weapon could bend, dent, or destroy. God was not just someone but *the* someone that David knew his heart could trust in, rely on, and lean on with confidence. Knowing this God was in his life, David was helped mentally, physically, emotional, and spiritually. This knowledge, this confidence and surety, this certainty of God made David's heart sing to Him in joyful praise!

Toward the end of his psalm (verse 8), David calls God his strength and stronghold, his source of power and security. Yet David also knows God isn't just his defender but a gentle leader who will nourish, shepherd, and carry His people forever (verse 9). David knew God was multidimensional—whoever David needed and claimed Him to be—in the moment.

Who is God to you today?

God, You are my all in all, what I need in every situation.
Be with me today, my shield, stronghold, strength, and shepherd.

ALL THE DIFFERENCE

But I am like an olive tree flourishing in the house of God;
I trust in God's unfailing love for ever and ever. For what you
have done I will always praise you in the presence of your faithful
people. And I will hope in your name, for your name is good.

PSALM 52:8–9 NIV

Have you ever had a glimpse into the life of a person who doesn't know Jesus? If so, you've probably seen the telltale signs. Someone who doesn't have a relationship with Christ lacks peace and purpose, hope and security, love and contentment. This person has a gaping emptiness that nothing in the world can fill, and yet they keep trying to fill it with stuff—only to grow even more dissatisfied and insecure. It's a vicious cycle of discontent.

Now contrast this with a Jesus-filled life—a life celebrated by the psalmist David, who compares himself to an olive tree, a tree known for its strength and resilience especially when faced with adverse weather conditions. The olive tree can survive things that most other plants and trees cannot. The olive tree is nothing if not resilient.

When you trust Christ as Lord and leader of your life, friend, you'll be resilient too! You'll be strong, productive, hopeful, loved, forgiven, joyful, and more! A life with Christ makes all the difference!

Lord of my life, I thank You. For saving me. For giving me
the gift of eternal life. For loving me without condition.

HOMESICK

*My soul longs, yes, faints for the courts of the Lord; my heart
and flesh sing for joy to the living God. Even the sparrow finds a
home, and the swallow a nest for herself, where she may lay her
young, at your altars, O Lord of hosts, my King and my God. . . .
For a day in your courts is better than a thousand elsewhere.*

PSALM 84:2–3, 10 ESV

There may be times when we find ourselves physically a long way from
our church. In those days away, we miss the people we worship with, the
pastor and his or her messages, and the time of fellowship that follows
after the service. We become homesick for our house of God, longing
for the intimacy we share between our fellow believers, our shepherd,
and our God.

Then, when we come back to town and return to our church home,
we rejoice that we are once again truly where we belong. We are back
in our spiritual nest where we are trained to imitate Jesus, to walk in the
Spirit, and soar as high as the eagle, forever upward toward our God.

Today praise God for giving you a church home, a place where you
can meet and greet God. A place where you can become the best version
of yourself, the best place you could ever be!

*Thank You, Lord, for my church home, where I can linger in
Your presence and rest under the shadow of Your wing.*

FOLLOW THE LEADER

On the day the tabernacle, the tent of the covenant law, was set up, the cloud covered it. From evening till morning the cloud above the tabernacle looked like fire. That is how it continued to be; the cloud covered it, and at night it looked like fire.

NUMBERS 9:15–16 NIV

Where are we headed? Who will lead us? When are we to move and go forward? And how far do we go? When are we to rest? And for how long do we rest?

Those are questions of the journey, questions that faced the Israelites on their march away from Egypt and from Sinai. But the Israelites are slowly but surely revealing themselves as a people of God. He is ever with them, and He is their God. God determined the answers to all the questions posed here. That cloud and that fire in union with the tent of the covenant governed their travel days and their days of rest. "At the LORD's command they encamped, and at the LORD's command they set out" (Numbers 9:23 NIV). The cloud and fire are things of beauty, representing a whole people living intimately with their Maker. They are God's people and He is their God.

Today consider how intimately you are living with your Maker.

Lord, reign in my heart like the cloud over the tent; take me wherever it is that You want me to go.

MERCY ME

Then, at the evening sacrifice, I rose from my self-abasement,
my tunic and cloak torn, and fell on my knees with my hands
spread out to the LORD my God and prayed: "I am too ashamed and
disgraced, my God, to lift up my face to you, because our sins are
higher than our heads and our guilt has reached to the heavens."
EZRA 9:5–6 NIV

Ezra was a man with many responsibilities. A Jewish scribe, he led a group of exiles from Judea to Jerusalem and tried hard to guide them to follow the teachings of God. Upon arriving in Jerusalem, however, he found that many had broken the laws set forth in the Torah and were otherwise living sinful lives.

Ezra took these things to heart. He seemed at his wit's end. Finally, he fell to his knees, splayed out before God, and prayed—not only for himself but for the people of Jerusalem. Before all, his voice alone resonated to God.

Ezra knew that God is merciful, and His mercy endures forever. You too can rest assured that no matter what your circumstances, God is listening and He is merciful. You just need to raise your prayers to Him, and He will listen.

Dear God, sometimes it is hard to know where to turn.
Sometimes I feel alone and scared. Please remind me to turn
my eyes to heaven and raise my voice to You in prayer.

YOU BELONG TO GOD

See what great love the Father has lavished on us, that we should be called children of God! And that is what we are! The reason the world does not know us is that it did not know him.

1 JOHN 3:1 NIV

If you're a parent, you know that there is no love greater than the love of a parent for a child. And yet in the frailty of our human condition, even we cannot love perfectly. But God, who is sovereign over all of creation, calls us His children. He loves us with a perfect, unconditional love. He knows us and He loves us still, enough to sacrifice His beloved Son on a cross that we might have life.

Our heavenly Father calls us sons and daughters. He calls us His own. We need not search for our identity in career or social status. Whether we are beautiful according to this world's standards or not makes no difference to our God. If others do not value you, that is because they do not value the almighty God.

Rest assured this day and each day that you live that your Father is watching over you. He knows your comings and your goings. He rejoices with you in victories and He shelters you with His wing when times are hard. He loves you and is a good, good Father.

Lord, remind me of my great worth because I belong to You. Amen.

HE SHALL

God shall arise, his enemies shall be scattered; and those who
hate him shall flee before him! . . . But the righteous shall be glad;
they shall exult before God; they shall be jubilant with joy!
PSALM 68:1, 3 ESV

Look around, and you might conclude that those who are against
God have the upper hand. Wickedness thrives, while God's ways are
dragged through the mud. You may wonder why God doesn't defend
His good name. In your heart, you may even be like James and John
who, after some Samaritan villagers rejected Jesus, said, "Lord, do you
want us to tell fire to come down from heaven and consume them?"
(Luke 9:54 ESV). But Jesus didn't turn to His disciples and say, "Yes!"
He rebuked them.

Once saved, your job on earth is not to avenge. What's more, you
don't have to fret over the state of your world today or any number
of tomorrows. You're to show the love and mercy of your Savior to a
generation of people who are against God and dying apart from Him.
You're to rest in the promise that at the right time, and with perfect
justice, God shall arise. He will take care of those who ultimately reject
Him, just as surely as He will care for those who receive righteousness
through His Son.

God, I was Your enemy, but now I am Your child.
Lead me to where I can share Your salvation with others.

HIS SWEET MERCY

We ourselves were once foolish, disobedient, led astray, slaves to various passions and pleasures, passing our days in malice and envy, hated by others and hating one another. But when the goodness and loving kindness of God our Savior appeared, he saved us, not because of works done by us in righteousness, but according to his own mercy, by the washing of regeneration and renewal of the Holy Spirit, whom he poured out on us richly through Jesus Christ our Savior.
TITUS 3:3–6 ESV

Mercy. What a beautiful word—it makes the whole of our being relax and smile. Since we are to think on good and lovely things in this life, then the concept of mercy should be one of those "things." How many times have people shown us grace? How many times have we extended compassion to others? Of course, the ultimate mercy is what God did for humankind through Jesus Christ.

Yes, God's sweet mercy came down from heaven and nothing in the world will ever, ever be the same again.

Dear God, I thank You for sending Your Son to die for me, to save me from my sins, to give me eternal life. I can never repay You for such a sacrifice, but I intend to serve You and love You for all time. Amen.

SECURITY BLANKET

*Grace (favor and spiritual blessing) to you and [heart]
peace from God our Father and the Lord Jesus Christ
(the Messiah, the Anointed One). Blessed be the God and
Father of our Lord Jesus Christ, the Father of sympathy
(pity and mercy) and the God [Who is the Source] of
every comfort (consolation and encouragement).*

2 CORINTHIANS 1:2–3 AMPC

There's something to be said for the feelings of serenity and security while snuggled in a plush comforter on a wintry day. You wrap yourself up in its warmth and feel at peace. Being enveloped in the loving arms of God is like that. He brings a feeling of serenity and peace to your heart that overcomes any trouble in your soul.

Each day, say a prayer of thanks for your blessings, beginning with the gift of Jesus Christ. For it's His presence that warms you from the inside out. He's a gift that no one can ever take away. With Jesus in your heart, you can face and do anything.

Praise God for the gift of His Son every day. Doing so will remind you that because Jesus is in your life, you're never alone. And His compassion, His love—they are all yours. Your gratitude and faith are all that's asked in exchange.

*God, Your love and warmth are my comfort and strength.
Thank You for the gift of Your Son, residing within my heart,
blessing me with peace and encouragement. Amen.*

A GOOD HEART

"Whatever is in your heart determines what you say.
A good person produces good things from the treasury
of a good heart, and an evil person produces evil
things from the treasury of an evil heart."
MATTHEW 12:34–35 NLT

Today's verses put forth a powerful message: whatever you have in your heart will determine what comes out of your mouth! Just as a contaminated well will bring forth contaminated water, so will a corrupted heart bring forth corrupted words.

So how does a woman make sure her words are pure and uplifting? By guarding her mind and heart in Christ: "Whatever is true, whatever is honorable, whatever is just, whatever is pure, whatever is lovely, whatever is commendable, if there is any excellence, if there is anything worthy of praise, think about these things" (Philippians 4:8 ESV).

To keep your heart and mind pure, be *intentional* every day about what you allow into your mind and heart. Turn away from whatever television, radio, online program, podcast, pundit, politician, parasite, pariah, party, or social media outlet is leading you away from humility, calm, and love, and turn toward the words and lessons of Jesus. Then you'll be heading the right way—God's way.

Lord, help me to truly follow You by not just loving and
caring for others more than myself but by thinking
only of things worthy of You and praise.

TEMPTING

*Jesus, full of the Holy Spirit, left the Jordan and
was led by the Spirit into the wilderness, where for
forty days he was tempted by the devil.*
LUKE 4:1–2 NIV

When we are in a time of wandering, lost in a desert, hungry, tired, or thirsty, the evil one strikes. He promises that all our problems will be fixed if we just step out of the path that God has prepared for us.

And it's so tempting to do. To live a life that's easier, calmer, more fulfilling according to worldly standards than the one God has put before us. Jesus knows what this temptation feels like, for the enemy tried Him in the literal desert.

Yet each time He was tempted, Jesus answered the devil's taunt with "It is written. . ." (Luke 4:4, 8, 12 NIV). For Jesus had God's promises stored in His heart. With them, He could repel and defeat the enemy's jabs with a single sentence.

We can do the same. Whether we're lost in the desert or on a mountain or enduring a season of sadness or joy, we too can have God's Word stored in our hearts so that when the enemy comes to tempt us, we'll know exactly what to say and what to do.

*God, thank You for giving me a way out of temptations.
Help me store Your Word in my heart. Amen.*

TRANSFORMATION PROCLAMATION

Sing to the LORD, all the earth! Tell of his salvation from day to day. Declare his glory among the nations, his marvelous works among all the peoples! For great is the LORD, and greatly to be praised, and he is to be feared above all gods.

1 CHRONICLES 16:22–25 ESV

Have you noticed a difference in your thought life or a change in your overall attitude since you became a believer? Chances are you have witnessed some improvements. Or maybe someone has told you she sees a change in you. Maybe certain situations just don't have the same effect on you as they once did.

When going through tests or trials, you may be tempted to entertain negative thoughts or adopt a bad attitude. If that happens, if your old ways begin to rise up in your heart and mind, rest assured that God sees you and He understands! He has compassion for you. And because of that compassion, He has a word for you, a scripture verse or a prayer, a transformation proclamation that you can write down, one that reminds you that you're a new creation. That the old way of thinking and reacting is gone. That you have been transformed by the renewing of your mind.

Lord, You are the great equipper. As I read Your Word, You transform my mind and attitude. As I pray, look upon me with compassion. Lead me out of all darkness and into Your light.

LIFE AND HEALTH

*He who is slow to anger has great understanding, but he who
is hasty of spirit exposes and exalts his folly. A calm and
undisturbed mind and heart are the life and health of the body,
but envy, jealousy, and wrath are like rottenness of the bones.*

PROVERBS 14:29–30 AMPC

How often has your temper gotten the best of you? How many times have
you wanted to take back the words you've said—even while they were
still tumbling out of your mouth? On what occasions has your health—
mentally, physically, emotionally, and spiritually—suffered because you
couldn't keep your cool within or without?

Proverbs reminds us we are to be slow to get angry. Instead, we
should try to understand people and situations. That we are to think
before we speak. That we are not to compare ourselves and our lives to
those of others but to enjoy where we are so that our mind and heart
will be calm, lacking in envy and anger, and our body will be healthy!

How do we get there from here? We continue in what we've learned,
what we truly and strongly believe. We keep our heads and hearts buried
in God's Word.

Let's begin today!

*Lord, help me to keep my entire being ensconced in Your truths,
precepts, love, and light. For when I am in You, I know I will find the
life and health, the peace and strength, the calm and cool I long for.*

THE VOICE OF THE LORD

The voice of the Lord is upon the waters; the God of glory thunders; the Lord is upon many (great) waters. The voice of the Lord is powerful; the voice of the Lord is full of majesty.

PSALM 29:3–4 AMPC

The Hebrew word used for "voice" in these verses has several shades of meaning. It can mean a roar, a scream, a growl, or a thunderbolt. It can also be a gentle jingle or the sweet sound of birds twittering.

We hear God in many ways. Sometimes He uses events in our lives that thunder like wild waves breaking on the shore—and sometimes He speaks to us in the still, small voice only we can hear. Either way, we need to be paying attention or we may miss what He is trying to tell us. This means listening for God's voice as we interact with the circumstances of our lives. It also means taking time to hear Him speaking to our hearts. As we learn to recognize God's voice, we can allow His Spirit to lead us into the actions He wants us to take.

Lord, make me sensitive, I pray, to Your voice. Help me never to be so busy that I forget to listen for what You are telling me. Then, having heard Your message to me, give me the strength and courage to act in ways that please You. Amen.

LEARNING TO REST IN HIM

*He shall not be afraid of evil tidings; his heart is firmly fixed,
trusting (leaning on and being confident) in the Lord.*

PSALM 112:7 AMPC

How often have you wanted God to open things up in your life and show you what He's working on? Just as the curious child is compelled to take something apart so she can look inside to see how it all works, you may have desired to see God at work, reassembling things in your life so that they come together better than before, working for your good.

Pause for a moment and look back on your life. What things could you have done better or perhaps just a little differently? What would it have looked like if you would have trusted the Lord more? What if you'd let go and given Him control, especially knowing Him better now than you knew Him then?

How had God faithfully put things back together for you in the past? What are some examples of His faithfulness to you and to your family? What changes could you make today in your thinking that would help you lean on and rest in Him even more when difficulties arise?

*Thank You, Lord, for always being at work in my life. Help me
walk by faith and rely on You even when I can't see all the details
ahead, knowing You're working things out for my good.*

JESUS IS A GENTLEMAN

"Here I am! I stand at the door and knock. If anyone
hears my voice and opens the door, I will come in
and eat with that person, and they with me."
REVELATION 3:20 NIV

Today's verse speaks of Jesus standing at the door of your heart and knocking. He does not and will not barge into your life and make Himself Lord over you—even though He could. Instead, Jesus chooses to be a gentleman. He waits. He longs for you to hear His call upon your life and open the door, but He will not push His way in. He wants you to open the door of your heart.

Maybe you have been a Christian for many years. You heard the call of the Lord and opened your heart to Him once upon a time. But since that time, you have forgotten about His presence in your life. You have become caught up in the world. Your career, family, and hobbies have overshadowed that true salvation experience. Take heart! It's never too late to return to the table with Jesus.

Just like a parent who is always glad to see his son at the door, coming home to share a meal, Jesus is always ready to reunite with you. Make your relationship with Christ a priority. Start today!

Jesus, I have missed our close fellowship. Join me at
the table. I long to walk closely with You again. Amen.

NOTHING IS BEYOND
HIS FORGIVENESS

[Jesus] said, "Do you see this woman? . . . She rained tears on my feet
and dried them with her hair. You gave me no greeting, but from the
time I arrived she hasn't quit kissing my feet. You provided nothing for
freshening up, but she has soothed my feet with perfume. Impressive, isn't
it? She was forgiven many, many sins, and so she is very, very grateful."
LUKE 7:44–47 MSG

As Christ-followers, we know nothing can keep us from God's love. *Not*
one single thing is beyond His forgiveness.

However, it's easy to fall into the trap of thinking that we're better
than those whose sin is "worse" than ours. That God must surely find
it difficult to forgive *those sinners*. That somehow our sins are superior,
right? Unfortunately, we don't always connect the dots from our heads
to our hearts to our actions.

Here in Luke 7, Jesus sets negative-thinking Simon straight. Simon
was focused on the weeping woman's past sins rather than her current
state of forgiveness. Jesus reminded Simon that he should instead focus
on a person's heart, a person's faith. That this woman's faith was beautiful,
her sins covered by God's amazing grace.

Ask God to help align your heart with your mind today.

Heavenly Father, I often have head knowledge that doesn't
make its way to my heart, words, and actions. I need
You to help me connect the dots. Thank You! Amen.

AN AGENT OF CHANGE

GOD is gracious—it is he who makes things right,
our most compassionate God. GOD takes the side
of the helpless; when I was at the end of my rope,
he saved me. I said to myself, "Relax and rest.
GOD has showered you with blessings."

PSALM 116:5–7 MSG

Looking for reasons to love the Lord? Check out Psalm 116 and you'll find a myriad of them!

You've a God who hears when you cry out (v. 1). He bends down close, listening intently as you pour your heart out to Him in prayer (v. 2). When troubles—spiritual or physical—seem to surround you, threatening your mental and emotional health, you can call out to a God who's gracious to you. The one who, in His compassion, will make things right (vv. 5–6). He comes alongside you, helping you when you feel helpless. He dries your tears and steadies your feet. He prompts you to relax and rest as you marvel at His showers of blessings (vv. 7–8).

All that God does to turn your life around gives you a new purpose and perspective, making you want to "give back to God. . .the blessings he's poured out on" you (v. 12 MSG). That, in turn, prompts you to reach out to others, to help transform their circumstances and perspectives as He works through you to make their lives a little more "right."

Lord, thank You for all the blessings that
make me an agent of change for You!

A MIGHTY GOD

When Jesus woke up, he rebuked the wind and
said to the waves, "Silence! Be still!" Suddenly the wind
stopped, and there was a great calm. Then he asked them,
"Why are you afraid? Do you still have no faith?"

MARK 4:39–40 NLT

Jesus had spent a long day preaching to the crowds, then explaining His teachings to His disciples. When evening set in, He suggested they leave the crowd and go by boat across the sea.

While Jesus slept in the stern, His head resting on a cushion, a storm came up. The wind howled and the waves grew, breaking over the boat and filling it with water. Panicked, the disciples came to Jesus, waking Him up and asking, "Don't you care that we're in such danger?"

Woman, Jesus knows that in this life you will have storms. In fact, He tells you to *expect* them (John 16:33). All He asks is that you not fear. For Jesus is already in your boat, riding the waves with you. Simply appeal to Him, and He will calm the storm with His words, "Silence! Be still!"

Remember: "Mightier than the violent raging of the seas, mightier than the breakers on the shore—the LORD above is mightier than these!" (Psalm 93:4 NLT). Never fear. God's got this.

Help me, Lord, to remember You have power and might over
all things—and are riding the waves of the storms with me.
With You in my boat, I need never be afraid! Amen.

REVIVED BY LOVE

I will worship toward Your holy temple and praise Your name
for Your loving-kindness and for Your truth and faithfulness;
for You have exalted above all else Your name and Your
word and You have magnified Your word above all Your name!

PSALM 138:2 AMPC

The psalmist knew what it was like to endure times of trouble and sorrow but to be confident to know that God would revive him (Psalm 138:7). He, like many that have come before and after him, may have wrestled with the challenges of life, endured great suffering, and sought solace.

The Word continually tells us that God saw the struggles of His people and spoke to them directly, through prophets, or through His Word. Sometimes He even transformed everyday challenges into extraordinary miracles.

You too may find there are seasons of life that are more laborious and taxing than others. Such times will stretch and refine your faith. While you're walking in them, remember that God loves you. Then turn your thoughts and heart toward the psalmist's words: "In the day when I called, You answered me; and You strengthened me with strength (might and inflexibility to temptation) in my inner self" (Psalm 138:3 AMPC).

Lord, "though I walk in the midst of trouble, You will revive me;
You will stretch forth Your hand against the wrath of my enemies,
and Your right hand will save me" (Psalm 138:7 AMPC).

GOD — SPEAK

We don't know what God wants us to pray for. But the Holy Spirit prays for us with groanings that cannot be expressed in words. And the Father who knows all hearts knows what the Spirit is saying, for the Spirit pleads for us believers in harmony with God's own will.

ROMANS 8:26–27 NLT

At times, you may not know how to put your request to God into words. Perhaps you've lost a dear loved one and are too stunned to adequately express yourself. It may be that some other event has left you without words.

In those situations, remember that even when you don't know what to say to God, the Holy Spirit is with you. As you wordlessly pray, He comes alongside and hears your groans and moans. He gets down to the heart of your matter and uncovers exactly how you feel, what you truly desire. He searches out and then transforms your "unspeakable yearnings and groanings too deep for utterance" (Romans 8:26 AMPC) into God-speak and brings them to the throne, pleading on your behalf "in harmony with God's will" (Romans 8:27 AMPC).

So don't let your not knowing what to say keep you from going to pray. Just sit before God, seeking His light with all your heart, soul, and mind. And let the Spirit take care of the rest.

Be with me, Holy Spirit. Search my heart and lift my wordless prayer to God's ear.

UNFAILING LOVE

*Lord, do not rebuke me in your anger or discipline me in
your wrath. Have mercy on me, Lord, for I am faint;
heal me, Lord, for my bones are in agony. My soul is in
deep anguish. How long, Lord, how long? Turn, Lord,
and deliver me; save me because of your unfailing love.*

PSALM 6:1–4 NIV

David was deeply anguished. Thoughts of his sinful state likely kept him up at night. His troubles weighed heavily on his soul. His words here in Psalm 6 reveal his absolute dread of God's anger and discipline. In fact, David begs for God's mercy.

And after airing his negative thoughts and feelings, David then acknowledges that God is fully capable of delivering him from his torment. Because God is a God of "unfailing love," David knows, without a doubt, that all will be well if it is God's will for his life. And that's that!

Like David, do thoughts of your sinful past interfere with a good night's sleep? Do your troubles weigh heavily on your spirit? Today is the day to approach the heavenly Father in bold confidence. Let Him know that you trust Him with the outcome. . .You trust Him to see you through to better days ahead. He will hear you, and He will act. Praise Him!

*Heavenly Father, I trust You for my comfort. . .
for deliverance from my troubles. Thank You for saving me!*

EVERYTHING SET RIGHT

I'm whistling, laughing, and jumping for joy; I'm singing your song,
High God. The day my enemies turned tail and ran, they stumbled
on you and fell on their faces. You took over and set everything
right; when I needed you, you were there, taking charge.

PSALM 9:1–4 MSG

In this psalm we find David singing praises to God, the doer of great things—the one who sets everything to right. David isn't praising half-heartedly, oh no. He's putting his *whole* heart and soul into it. He's "whistling, laughing, and jumping for joy." His *entire being* is directed in praise to Almighty God.

We can experience this same kind of bubbling-up joy that David did. Because when hard times come. . .when nothing is going our way. . .we can trust our heavenly Father with the outcome. He can—He *will*—transform our troubles. He knows just what we need. And if we give control over to Him, He'll set everything right in His perfect timing.

Ask God to take charge of your life, starting right this very minute. And once He begins to work, remember how He is always there when you need Him. Share with others the great things He has done for you. Telling of God's awesomeness. . .what a wonderful way to praise Him!

Today, I ask You to take complete charge of my life, Lord. No matter what, You are always the one who can set things right. I praise You!

A SURE FAITH

A centurion came to [Jesus]. . . . "Lord," he said, "my servant lies at home paralyzed, suffering terribly." Jesus said to him, "Shall I come and heal him?" The centurion replied, "Lord, I do not deserve to have you come under my roof. But just say the word, and my servant will be healed. For I myself am a man under authority, with soldiers under me. I tell this one, 'Go,' and he goes; and that one, 'Come,' and he comes. I say to my servant, 'Do this,' and he does it." When Jesus heard this, he was amazed and said to those following him, "Truly I tell you, I have not found anyone in Israel with such great faith."

MATTHEW 8:5–10 NIV

"*Just say the word*, and my servant will be healed," the centurion said to Jesus. Can you imagine a greater, surer faith than that? Just *a word* was all he asked for. . .nothing more, nothing less.

The centurion didn't ask Jesus for some fancy, elaborate ceremony. He didn't even ask Jesus to come to his house! And Jesus' response? Amazement! In fact, the Bible tells us that Jesus hadn't found a single person in all of Israel who displayed that kind of sure faith.

As a Christ follower, do you have a sure faith? . . . The heavenly Father will assure your uncertain heart today! Just ask!

Father, I thank You for Your Word that gives me blessed assurance!

RESTLESS NIGHTS

*The king had trouble sleeping, so he ordered an attendant
to bring the book of the history of his reign so it could be read
to him. In those records he discovered an account of how
Mordecai had exposed the plot. . .to assassinate King Xerxes.*
ESTHER 6:1–2 NLT

Queen Esther's cousin Mordecai, a Jew, refused to bow down to anyone other than God. This enraged the honor-craving Haman, a servant of King Xerxes. So Haman urged the king to send out a decree to annihilate the Jews. Later he went a step further and had a gallows built on which he planned to have Mordecai hanged.

That night, King Xerxes had trouble sleeping. He was so restless, he had someone read the memoirs of his reign. That's when he learned Mordecai had once saved his life and hadn't been recognized.

From that point on, God ended up turning things around, changing circumstances in a profound way. For that night, the king decided to honor Mordecai. . .and later commanded that Haman be executed on the very gallows he'd had built for Mordecai's demise!

God has a way of reaching us, of getting our attention by any means available. When you find yourself persistently restless, spend some time before God. Go deep. Ask Him what He wants you to know, to do. Then watch how God begins to turn things around.

*Lord, You have my full attention. What do You want me
to know, to do, to help You turn circumstances around?*

PROMISE OF HEAVEN

Break the arms of these wicked, evil people! Go after them until the last one is destroyed. The LORD is king forever and ever! The godless nations will vanish from the land. LORD, you know the hopes of the helpless. Surely you will hear their cries and comfort them. You will bring justice to the orphans and the oppressed, so mere people can no longer terrify them.

PSALM 10:15–18 NLT

Have you ever felt completely and utterly helpless because of the hurt someone has caused you? Just. . .stuck. With nowhere to turn?

Maybe you've been bullied, cheated on, beat down by someone you love or by an acquaintance or even a stranger. And maybe you felt like no one had your back. No one was there to pick you up, dust you off, and breathe new life into your weary soul. If this is part of your story, sister, there is hope! As Psalm 10 states: "LORD, you know the hopes of the helpless. Surely you will hear their cries and comfort them."

And this same Lord Jesus promises to deliver you today. For He is your rescuer. . .the justice-bringer. When you know Him as Your Lord and Savior, you never need to feel helpless or hopeless again. Thank Him today for bringing you peace and comfort. . .for offering the ultimate deliverance from hard things—heaven, your glorious and final destination!

Lord Jesus, I look forward to the promise of heaven!

PRAYING FOR PEACE

Pray for the peace of Jerusalem:
"May those who love you be secure."
PSALM 122:6 NIV

With the news of yet another outbreak of unrest in the Middle East, this phrase comes to mind: "Pray for the peace of Jerusalem." One might think that King David had prophetically understood how war torn this area of the world would be over the centuries. And, while it is good for us to pray for peace from war in Jerusalem and other places in the world, we should also be praying for peace with God.

As the Prince of Peace, Jesus overcame the world—its wars, pain, and evil. Jesus is the way to peace, both our inner peace and the peace of the world. But it all begins with us as we seek God's will for our lives; get closer to Him; quiet our minds; and listen to that still, small voice. There can be no lasting peace anywhere without being renewed day by day, praying for inner peace, growth of grace, and the love of ourselves and others.

Dear Father, thank You for sending the Prince of Peace to be our peace. Let me be a peacemaker by praying for peace for Jerusalem and elsewhere. I pray that I can be an instrument of Your peace and show love so that others will seek to love You with all their hearts. You are the God of peace; bless me with Your peace forever. Amen.

COURAGEOUS FAITH

Just then a woman who had hemorrhaged for twelve years slipped in from behind and lightly touched his robe. She was thinking to herself, "If I can just put a finger on his robe, I'll get well." Jesus turned—caught her at it. Then he reassured her: "Courage, daughter. You took a risk of faith, and now you're well." The woman was well from then on.

MATTHEW 9:20–22 MSG

This woman mentioned in Matthew 9 had suffered from a health issue for twelve long years. She had likely spent everything she had on doctors, who weren't able to heal her or even improve her bleeding issue. We can imagine that she was most certainly desperate. . .maybe on the verge of beyond hope.

But. . .Jesus. This woman's powerful combination of persistence and courage led her to take action—and in the crowd that followed Jesus, she reached out her arm to Him and touched His robe. And in that moment, she was healed from her bleeding issue.

When we know Jesus, we can *always* have a courageous faith. No matter what we're in need of, all we need to do is reach out to Him. And He will reassure us that all will be fine because He's there to see us through. Praise Him!

Father God, thank You for the courageous displays of faith I can read about in Your Word. I'm done playing it safe. Starting today. . .I will be courageous in my faith!

PURE AND UNCHANGING

Into the hovels of the poor, into the dark streets where the
homeless groan, God speaks: "I've had enough; I'm on my way
to heal the ache in the heart of the wretched." God's words
are pure words, pure silver words refined seven times in the
fires of his word-kiln, pure on earth as well as in heaven.

PSALM 12:5–8 MSG

If you've lived any amount of time on this earth, it's certain that another human being—a friend, a family member, a coworker—has let you down because of his or her empty promises. And, just as likely, you've disappointed someone in your life as well. As humans, we're often quick to make a promise and just as quick to fail in the follow-through.

But thankfully, when we've accepted Christ as our Lord and Savior, we can say with confidence, "He will never let us down." He's in the business of promise-keeping; His promises are a sure thing. His words are pure.

The truth is:

Humans aren't trustworthy. . . God is.

Humans aren't faithful. . . God is.

Humans are promise-breakers. . . God is a promise-keeper.

Humans will fail us. . . God won't!

Where men and women fall short, God *always* comes through. His Word is pure and unchanging.

Promise-keeper, my Savior, I trust in You alone. You are
all that is pure and right in the world. Thank You for
being true to Your Word. You never let me down!

MORE JESUS

"Are you tired? Worn out? Burned out on religion?
Come to me. Get away with me and you'll recover your life.
I'll show you how to take a real rest. Walk with me and work
with me—watch how I do it. Learn the unforced rhythms of
grace. I won't lay anything heavy or ill-fitting on you. Keep
company with me and you'll learn to live freely and lightly."
MATTHEW 11:28–30 MSG

When was the last time you had a real, honest-to-goodness rest? . . .
The kind that refreshes you both mentally and physically. . . Rest that
makes you feel completely revitalized and alive!

If that sounds like wishful thinking. . .if your mind tells you, *Yeah,*
right! I haven't had a good rest in at least ten years—and there's no end in
sight for me! . . .take these words from Matthew 11 to heart. Jesus says,
"Get away with me. . . . I'll show you how to take a real rest." What a
promise!

Instead of more *busy* in your life, get more of *Jesus*. He is just what
your weary soul needs. He will pull you from the depths of your day-
to-day burnout and give you rest like you've never experienced it
before—a rest that leads to free and light living! Praise Him!

Father God, rest-giver, comfort my world-weary
soul today. I am exhausted! I trust You to show
me the way to refreshing rest. Thank You!

YOU ARE LOVED

Love is patient, love is kind. It does not envy, it does not boast, it is not proud. It does not dishonor others, it is not self-seeking, it is not easily angered, it keeps no record of wrongs. Love does not delight in evil but rejoices with the truth.

1 CORINTHIANS 13:4–6 NIV

We may not have great success at implementing this impressive list of love's qualities. God, however, never fails at loving us completely and enduringly. All our lives, He has loved us with patience and kindness. And although the people around us may also fail to meet God's high standard of love, He does not. He is never irritable or resentful with us and rejoices over us when we make good choices.

Understanding how God sees us is critical to our trusting Him. Sometimes our brain tells us we're trusting when our emotions are still fearful. That's because head knowledge is different from heart knowledge. It's when our hearts are satisfied that His affection doesn't waver that we can trust God completely.

Take a deep breath and relax in the truth that God is good and you can trust Him with every part of your life: your family, work, relationships, health, and more. Look back over your life and remember the ways God has proven His great love for you. Rest in His affection today.

God, thank You for your perfect love.
Help me to let go of fear and trust You.

KNOWING HE WILL ANSWER

I am praying to you because I know you will answer, O God.
Bend down and listen as I pray. Show me your unfailing love in
wonderful ways. By your mighty power you rescue those who
seek refuge from their enemies. Guard me as you would guard
your own eyes. Hide me in the shadow of your wings.
PSALM 17:6–8 NLT

"Bend down and listen as I pray. . . ," says the psalmist, who expresses his expectation that God will answer him. He trusts that the heavenly Father's love for him is so big, so guaranteed. . .that nothing—absolutely *nothing*—can get in the way of that.

Imagine God bending down from heaven, intently looking you in the eye—you have His full attention—He's focused and waiting to hear what you have to share with Him. Now, get this: that's what praying to Him is really like. He is *that* focused on you, sister! Talking with Him is like having a conversation with a friend who's the best listener on earth.

So if you've ever questioned whether the Father hears everything that's on your heart, ask Him to assure your spirit—to help you move from uncertain to knowing. Then thank Him for His love, which is bigger than anything you could ever imagine.

Heavenly Father, thank You for being the best listener a girl could ever hope for. . .thank You for helping to grow my trust in Your unfailing love!

BEAUTIFUL BEGINNINGS

GOD made my life complete when I placed all the pieces
before him. When I got my act together, he gave me a fresh start.
Now I'm alert to GOD's ways; I don't take God for granted.
Every day I review the ways he works; I try not to miss a trick.
I feel put back together, and I'm watching my step. GOD rewrote
the text of my life when I opened the book of my heart to his eyes.
PSALM 18:20–24 MSG

Think about where you are in your life's story. Are the chapters before you met Jesus overflowing with one hot mess after another? Bad choices? Jumbled thoughts? Unclear direction? If so, what about *after*?

While life with Jesus certainly isn't all sunshine, rainbows, and unicorns, this new way of living does have it perks. With God in the lead, you always have a guide to help you navigate the messiness of life. You have someone by your side to help you make sense of the madness. . . to turn your chaos into peace.

Truth is, God's story for you is so much better than anything you could ever write on your own. So don't attempt to write it all by yourself. Make sure you hand over the writing to the heavenly author Himself. He'll see to it that your story of transformation has a beautiful, eternal theme of hope and security.

Father, thank You for rewriting my life story!

NOTHING BUT GOOD PLANS

In times of trouble, may the LORD answer your cry. May the name of the God of Jacob keep you safe from all harm. May he send you help from his sanctuary and strengthen you from Jerusalem. May he remember all your gifts and look favorably on your burnt offerings. May he grant your heart's desires and make all your plans succeed. May we shout for joy when we hear of your victory and raise a victory banner in the name of our God. May the LORD answer all your prayers.
PSALM 20:1–5 NLT

Do you believe 100 percent, without a doubt, that the heavenly Father will answer *all* your prayers? Not that He will say *yes* to your every request—but that He will answer with a yes, no, or maybe later?

Whether you're asking God for hope, healing, help, or safety from harm, you can know with certainty that He will do what's best for you—He has nothing but good plans for you, sister! His promise in Jeremiah 29:11 (NIV) says, "For I know the plans I have for you. . .plans to prosper you and not to harm you, plans to give you a hope and a future."

So pray with complete confidence to the one who offers protection, strength, hope, success and know that an answer is coming your way!

Heavenly Father, You love me and want only the best for me. Thank You for Your answers to my prayers!

PERFECTLY IN STEP

Clear my name, GOD; I've kept an honest shop. I've thrown in my lot with you, GOD, and I'm not budging. Examine me, GOD, from head to foot, order your battery of tests. Make sure I'm fit inside and out so I never lose sight of your love, but keep in step with you, never missing a beat.

PSALM 26:1–3 MSG

While he certainly hadn't lived a perfect life, the psalmist David was confident that he had walked in the Lord's truth. He had a genuine trust and ever-growing relationship with his heavenly Father. And so he requested that God examine him—he wanted to be sure that he was spiritually fit. He knew that keeping in step with the Lord's plan would help him to fully experience the love of Christ, while "never missing a beat."

So, dear one, what does this mean for you? If you've accepted Jesus Christ as Lord and leader of Your life, you share a bond with Him that can never be broken. Simply trust Him to keep your spiritual "fitness" in check, and you'll never lose sight of His amazing, unconditional love. You can be confident that, no matter what life brings, the Lord will keep you on the right path—staying in step with Him—so you won't waver in your Christian journey.

Father, examine me. . .know my heart. I long to keep in step with You today and all my days to come.

A GOD-CENTERED LIFE

Except the Lord builds the house, they labor in vain who build it;
except the Lord keeps the city, the watchman wakes but in vain.
It is vain for you to rise up early, to take rest late, to eat the bread
of [anxious] toil—for He gives [blessings] to His beloved in sleep.
PSALM 127:1–2 AMPC

God wants to be involved in every aspect of your life. Your home, work, play, family, church, neighborhood, and country. When He is, you get closer to what He intends, not just for you but for the people around you.

At the same time, God wants you not to work yourself to the bone nor to be anxious about the results of your endeavors. Instead, you are to leave all outcomes of your efforts to Him.

The Lord knows that a life lived without Him at the center is a life not worth living. So be sure to put God in the center of your processes as you build your life with Him by your side. As you do so, you will find yourself blessed with peace and so much more, including a good night's rest.

Lord, too often I get so wrapped up in my work, family,
and church that I forget to include You in the process.
Remind me each day to look to You for all things, to do my
best in all endeavors, and to leave all the results to You.

GOD'S LOVE SONG

*"The LORD your God is with you, the Mighty Warrior who
saves. He will take great delight in you; in his love he will
no longer rebuke you, but will rejoice over you with singing."*
ZEPHANIAH 3:17 NIV

Read Zephaniah 3:17, and you will find a verse packed with God's love. First, this verse reminds God's children that He is always with them. Wherever they go, whatever they do, in every situation, God watches over them with Fatherly love. Next, it says that God's love is not just ever-present but also all-powerful. When bad things happen, God's children needn't ask, "Where is God?" They can be confident that their Father is present with a mighty plan to save them. The verse continues on, conveying God's gentleness in love. He quiets His children. His love is like a soft, soothing lullaby sung by a mother to her child. It brings His children comfort and peace. The verse ends with God singing. Yes, God sings! The Bible says in Zephaniah 3:17 that God rejoices over His children with singing. Isn't that amazing? God takes such delight in His children that He cannot contain His love for them. His love bursts forth in joyous song.

From beginning to end, this little piece of scripture is God's love song to His children. You are His child. Read it often and know that He loves you.

*Dear God, thank You for loving me fully,
unconditionally, and always. Amen.*

PRAISE THE BLESSING-GIVER

"So obey the commands of the LORD your God by walking in his ways and fearing him. For the LORD your God is bringing you into a good land of flowing streams and pools of water, with fountains and springs. . . . It is a land of wheat and barley; of grapevines, fig trees, and pomegranates; of olive oil and honey. It is a land where food is plentiful. . . . When you have eaten your fill, be sure to praise the LORD your God for the good land he has given you."

DEUTERONOMY 8:6–10 NLT

When we obey God, we're often blessed with a good life. And while our lives are not entirely free from hardship, the heavenly Father gifts us with blessings—often too numerous to count!

Though wonderful, our seasons of success and abundance should come with a warning. During easy times, we can become distracted from the true blessing-giver. And we might even become prideful, convinced we're deserving of it all.

Remember these words from Deuteronomy; soak them up in your mind and your heart. Life—the good life!—comes from God and God alone. He is the miracle worker, the keeper of promises, the one who saves! He is worthy to be praised!

Blessing-giver, thank You for this beautiful, full life.
Help me to always remember that I could have none of
these blessings without You. You are so, so good to me! Amen.

GOD OF ALL THE EARTH

Shout for joy to God, all the earth; sing the glory of his name; give to him glorious praise! Say to God, "How awesome are your deeds! So great is your power that your enemies come cringing to you. All the earth worships you and sings praises to you."

PSALM 66:1–4 ESV

Do you tend to reserve your songs of praise for Sunday morning? Or do you sing praises for God's goodness throughout the week too?

In the verses above, the psalmist is calling *everyone* to joyfully praise God—after all, God is the God over all the earth—not just the God of Israel. The psalmist then follows with instruction on *how* to praise God: "Say to God, 'How awesome are your deeds!'" Praise involves telling God how amazing He is. . .what wonderful things He has done in your life. . . Praise celebrates His awesome power.

If praise doesn't come easily or naturally because your mind runs amok with thoughts of doubt and fear, ask God to remind you that He's in control and will protect and care for you always. When you invite Him to take complete control, your worries will be replaced with joy—and, as thoughts of thanksgiving and hope fill your mind, praise will spill from your heart and lips!

Father God, You are God of all the earth. And I am so thankful. I will praise You every day of my life! Amen.

NEGATIVE TO POSITIVE

If I had not confessed the sin in my heart, the Lord would not have listened. But God did listen! He paid attention to my prayer. Praise God, who did not ignore my prayer or withdraw his unfailing love from me.

PSALM 66:18–20 NLT

Sometimes our thoughts lie. Our mind fills to overflowing with negative messages:

I'm not good enough.   *God doesn't love me.*
I'm boring.   *And He certainly doesn't care*
I'm not talented.   *about anything I have to say.*

Tune out those negative thoughts! Have a heart-to-heart with God today. Ask Him to help drown out your negative thinking. Ask Him to replace the lies with truths like:

Because of God's love and grace, I am good enough.
God created me to be interesting, talented, and smart.
God loves me in a BIG way!
And He cares about every single thing I have to say!

No matter what your brain tries to tell you, God is faithful, and He loves you more than you could ever imagine. Tell God exactly what you're thinking and feeling. Confess the sin in your heart and keep your focus wholly on Him. . .and He will be 100 percent tuned in to your prayers.

Father, I praise You! Thank You for loving me perfectly.
Please take control of my thoughts. Help me to let go
of the negative and focus on the positive. Amen.

SHEEP SEEKER

For thus saith the Lord GOD; Behold, I, even I, will both search
my sheep, and seek them out. As a shepherd seeketh out his
flock in the day that he is among his sheep that are scattered;
so will I seek out my sheep, and will deliver them out of all places
where they have been scattered in the cloudy and dark day.

EZEKIEL 34:11–12 KJV

The Lord spoke through Ezekiel about His love for people. He shared about how God pursues them, seeks them out. Even today, God still seeks out His beloved children.

In this moment, reflect on God's love. Recall when you began a relationship with Him. Meditate on some of today's readings to remind you of God's grace and mercy upon you. For example, Proverbs 21:2–3 (NIV) says: "A person may think their own ways are right, but the LORD weighs the heart. To do what is right and just is more acceptable to the LORD than sacrifice."

God isn't looking for more sacrifice—He already took care of that on the cross. God isn't looking for you to save yourself or put yourself in right standing with Him—He also took care of that on the cross. God just wants you, imperfections and all, to trust Him. Enter His sheep-seeker arms and rest.

Father, as a child snuggles up with a stuffed animal, may I feel
Your warmth and presence in a way I never have before.

BLOOMING GLORY

The desert and the parched land will be glad;
the wilderness will rejoice and blossom.
ISAIAH 35:1 NIV

Come to the desert on one day and you'll find dry, cracked earth, with not a drop of moisture in sight. The sun will beat down, driving you to find any tiny bit of shade. Signs of life will be scarce as every animal tries to conserve energy and hide from the overwhelming weight of heat.

But then the rains come.

And the next day, in the space of hours, spores burst forth, blooms open, and a great hallelujah of light and life explodes into sight with all the beauty of the rainbow. Like a painter's palette fresh from a masterpiece, vibrant hues cover the drab background. The earth rejoices!

The same change can occur in your life. Once thirsty for meaning, you can find soul refreshment in Him. Once parched and weary, weighed down with the monotony of life, you can find purpose in His plan. Once aching for relief, you can rest in the glorious pleasure of His forgiveness and grace.

Your God is the one who can strengthen the feeble and steady the unstable. He's the one who can turn fear into courage and doubt into bravery. He's the one who can open blind eyes, unstop deaf ears, and cause mute tongues to shout for joy (Isaiah 35:3–6). And for all this and more, you follow Him.

Lord, thank You for glorious change. Amen.

PEACE, PLEASE!

"Peace I leave with you; my peace I give to you. Not as the world gives do I give to you. Let not your hearts be troubled, neither let them be afraid."

JOHN 14:27 ESV

What is peace? Peace can mean freedom from conflict between nations. Peace can mean harmony among people. Peace can mean calmness following chaos.

But the peace Jesus spoke about goes beyond the peace of this world. Our world is broken, so any peace we create by human effort is fragile. Not so with Jesus' peace. Jesus' peace means conflict and animosity and chaos can happen all around us, yet we remain secure, unafraid, and calm. How is *that* kind of peace possible?

Only through Christ. He can accomplish in us what we cannot do ourselves. Jesus even said, "Apart from me you can do *nothing*" (John 15:5 ESV, emphasis added). The opposite also holds true: when we abide in Him, nothing is out of our reach, including peace in our hearts.

Life may be like a smooth sea for you right now. But maybe there's something on the horizon or already surrounding you that's lapping at your peace. Abide in Jesus. Stay close to Him. He's holding out His peace. It's yours for the taking. So grab hold!

Lord, I've been relying on the peace the world gives, and it's no surprise my heart is troubled. Thank You for the peace You offer—peace that is ever possible.

URGENT!

"First things first. . . . Announce God's kingdom!"
. . . Jesus said, "No procrastination. . . . You can't
put God's kingdom off till tomorrow. Seize the day."
LUKE 9:60, 62 MSG

Maybe you've heard the phrase, "Don't put off until tomorrow what you can do today." It rings true, doesn't it?

Those dishes in the sink. . .the piles of dirty laundry. . .the ever-growing grass. . .the flowerbeds overrun with weeds. . . Whatever you put off today will still need to be done tomorrow. So "Don't put off until tomorrow" is pretty good advice, isn't it?

God's Word is also full of timeless, practical advice. And today's verses from the book of Luke are no exception. Here Jesus emphasizes the urgency of doing the most important thing first: growing God's kingdom! When we commit our lives to Christ, our priority should be Him—and that means sharing Him with others. Our commitment to Him can't be 80 percent; it needs to be 100 percent, with no distractions.

The challenge is the noisy world that tempts us away from God's calling on our lives. So what's a woman of God to do? Look up! Ask the heavenly Father to keep your mind- and heart-focus on Him and Him alone. He won't let you down!

Father God, I humbly come before You, asking You
to help me keep my mind- and heart-focus on You.
I want to help grow Your kingdom, Lord! Amen.

SOUL, STRENGTH, AND MIND

" 'Love the Lord your God with all your heart and with all your soul and with all your strength and with all your mind'; and, 'Love your neighbor as yourself.' "

<small>LUKE 10:27 NIV</small>

Love my neighbor as I love myself? But I don't even "like" my neighbor. Surely, I can do something else, can't I, Lord? I mean, even a root canal sounds more appealing.

Is there any other biblical command that seems more difficult than "love your neighbor"? It's hard enough to love our families and friends when we're having a bad day. But the truth of the matter is, if we love Jesus with everything we have (our heart, soul, strength, and mind), then our actions will show it! And that includes loving others well. Jesus loved. . .*loves*. . .each of us even at our very worst, doesn't He? So who are we to deny loving-kindness to others? Even those who are hardest to love?

Today, take a moment to reflect on these verses from Luke 10. Ask the Lord to soften your heart, to strengthen your mind, and to change your thinking toward your hard-to-love neighbors. God, the promise-keeper, will hear. He will respond. He will write love all over your heart and soul.

Father God, thank You for being the best example of how to love others well. Change my mindset. Show me that I can love people who seem unlovable. Amen.

WIDE–EYED WONDER

*"No one lights a lamp, then hides it in a drawer. It's put on a lamp
stand so those entering the room have light to see where they're going.
. . . If you live wide-eyed in wonder and belief, your body fills up with
light. If you live squinty-eyed in greed and distrust, your body is a musty
cellar. Keep your eyes open, your lamp burning, so you don't get musty
and murky. Keep your life as well-lighted as your best-lighted room."*
LUKE 11:33–36 MSG

A light that remains unseen can't brighten a dark room. It can't illuminate
a shadowy path. A hidden light serves no purpose.

The same is true of our faith. If we keep the light of our faith hidden,
we're doing the world—our friends, neighbors, and strangers—a grave
disservice.

The best way to fill yourself with God's radiant light is to open your
eyes to His wonders:

*I'm thanking you, GOD, from a full heart, I'm writing
the book on your wonders. I'm whistling, laughing,
and jumping for joy; I'm singing your song, High God.*
PSALM 9:1–2 MSG

So keep your soul and mind focused on the goodness of God. . .on
His unending mercy and blessings. When you stay tuned in to the pos-
itives, your light will grow a little brighter every day. And the beauty of
it all is that you will draw others into the light.

God, open my eyes to Your awesome wonders. Amen.

THE WORRY—FREE LIFE

*Jesus said. . . , "Therefore I tell you, do not worry about your
life, what you will eat; or about your body, what you will wear.
For life is more than food, and the body more than clothes.
Consider the ravens: They do not sow or reap, they have no
storeroom or barn; yet God feeds them. . . . Who of you by
worrying can add a single hour to your life? Since you cannot
do this very little thing, why do you worry about the rest?*

LUKE 12:22–26 NIV

What if someone else could handle the stresses and worries of your
health, finances, relationships, work, politics—*all the things* that cause
those pesky worry and frown lines to crease your forehead? No doubt
you'd like to imagine what a worry-free life feels like.

Here's the beautiful thing: not only can you imagine it. . .you can
actually *live* it! How? By giving every anxiety-inducing thought to Jesus.

The direction of your life will always mirror your strongest thoughts
(see Proverbs 4:23)—and if those thoughts are worry-filled, you'll never
be able to escape overwhelming fear and anxiety. When you create new
pathways of thought, fully trusting the heavenly Father with your life,
then this positive way of thinking will become your default. And the
worry-free life will be yours for the taking!

*Jesus, help me redirect my worried thoughts and fully
trust You in the process. Thank You, Lord! Amen.*

BECAUSE HE'S GOD!

Let those on the hunt for you sing and celebrate. Let all who
love your saving way say over and over, "God is mighty!"

PSALM 70:4 MSG

David is calling all God's people to be happy in Him and to sing His praises. He doesn't put any stipulations on it: "*If* God makes your life perfect. . ." or "*If* God answers your prayers the way you'd like Him to. . ." or "*If* God blesses you financially. . ." There are no "ifs"—no requirements are attached to David's directive. God's people should be joyful solely *because He's God*!

Today let your thoughts rest on the character of God. He is good. He is holy. He is just. He is infinite. He is patient. He is faithful. He is love. He is forgiving. He is creative. He is truth. He is welcoming. . .and so much more! Spend some time in His Word, and you'll realize that God is worthy of your love and praise just because of who He is.

When you focus on how good God is (all the time!), you'll find your heart growing more grateful, more content, more joyful. And when your heart is overflowing with joy, positivity will trickle into every area of your life. Say it out loud: "God is mighty!"

God, You are mighty! You are so, so good to me. I am so grateful
to have You in my heart and in my life. I praise You! Amen.

LEAN ON ME

LORD, I seek refuge in You. . . . In Your justice, rescue and deliver me; listen closely to me and save me. Be a rock of refuge for me, where I can always go. Give the command to save me. . . . Deliver me, my God, from the power of the wicked. . . . For You are my hope, Lord GOD, my confidence from my youth. I have leaned on You from birth. . . . My praise is always about You.

PSALM 71:1–6 HCSB

We all need someone to lean on when life throws us a curveball. No matter how close we walk with God, He doesn't guarantee a trouble-free life (John 16:33). And when trouble comes, it's difficult to face the struggle alone.

When trouble comes in the form of a health scare. . .a financial crisis . . .a strained relationship. . .who is your go-to person? Our brains often train us to first approach a friend, family member, professional counselor, or other "expert" for help. But our first "go-to" should be the one who provides refuge, deliverance, and support through *all* life's trials. The heavenly Father is significant to our physical and mental well-being.

So when you need someone to lean on, recall this passage from the Psalms—and call out to the one who handles your heart with the very best care!

God, when life is hard, remind me that I can always lean on You! Amen.

RESTORATION

Your righteousness, God, reaches to the heavens, you who have done great things. Who is like you, God? Though you have made me see troubles, many and bitter, you will restore my life again; from the depths of the earth you will again bring me up. You will increase my honor and comfort me once more.

PSALM 71:19–21 NIV

Ever felt like the walls are closing in around you? No matter which way you look, you can't see a way out. You feel like you're beyond all hope. Your life is a wreck. And you're left wondering if it's beyond repair.

Although it doesn't seem possible, when you feel hopeless, you are presented with a wonderful opportunity. Because the very best way to grow your faith and increase your trust in God is through your trials. Whatever hardships you encounter in life, they all present you with delightful moments to recognize and embrace God's deliverance and grace. The God who heals (Jeremiah 17:14) offers complete restoration for your heart and soul.

The more your heart and mind are tuned to the heavenly Father's deliverance, the more you'll be able to release your bitter thoughts and burdens to Him. Just try it! You'll be so glad you did! Your thoughts and your soul will thank you! Ask the heavenly Father for His healing restoration today!

Father, restore my heart. Restore my hope. Thank You for taking my broken life, giving me healing, and covering me with Your grace. Amen.

ABSOLUTELY NOTHING

For I am convinced that neither death nor life, neither angels
nor demons, neither the present nor the future, nor any powers,
neither height nor depth, nor anything else in all creation, will be able
to separate us from the love of God that is in Christ Jesus our Lord.
ROMANS 8:38–39 NIV

Sometimes, when our circumstances spiral downward and we feel like we're living a nightmare, we wonder where God went. His love, which is supposed to be never-ending, seems out of reach. We pray, but our words seem to bounce off the ceiling and fall flat on the floor.

But it doesn't matter how we feel. God promised that nothing can separate us from His overwhelming, magnificent, powerful love. And though our circumstances may numb our sensors, making it seem like His love is absent, we can fall back on faith in God's promises. His love is there, enveloping us, whether we feel it or not. Nothing in this world can keep His love from us. Absolutely nothing.

Cancer may destroy our flesh, but it won't destroy God's love. Bills may deplete our finances, but they can't deplete His love. Relationships may break our hearts, but they will never break His love. We don't have to face any of life's difficulties alone, for our Creator loves us. He will hold our hands through it all. And when we are too weak to face another day, His love will carry us.

Dear Father, help me to rest in Your constant, steadfast love. Amen.

ARE YOU REALLY LISTENING?

"Simply put, if you're not willing to take what is dearest to you, whether plans or people, and kiss it good-bye, you can't be my disciple. Salt is excellent. But if the salt goes flat, it's useless, good for nothing. Are you listening to this? Really listening?"
LUKE 14:33–35 MSG

What are you willing to give up for Jesus? Would you be willing to walk away from everything most important to you? Your family? Your friends? Your home? Your job? Your future plans? It might be easy to give up some things you *like*. But those you *love*?

Jesus doesn't mince words when it comes to following Him and being committed to Him. He is uncompromising in what He asks of His disciples. And so, there have been many who have chosen to walk away. But. . .those who really understand what He offers, they stay.

When you recognize that He is love. . .He is life. . .He is *everything* you'll ever need. When the truth of His Word sinks deep into your heart, you can't help but follow Him wholly, with everything you have. You'll walk away from everything to follow Him.

You can't have other priorities that the Lord has to compete with. . . no! He alone must be your priority. Are you listening? Won't you stay?

*Jesus, I am listening. I will stay and follow
You. You alone are my priority. Amen.*

EVERYTHING YOU ARE, EVERYTHING YOU HAVE

"Be vigilant in keeping the Commandment and The Revelation that Moses the servant of GOD laid on you: Love GOD, your God, walk in all his ways, do what he's commanded, embrace him, serve him with everything you are and have."
JOSHUA 22:5 MSG

"Be vigilant," begins Joshua in his directive to the eastern tribes. They had just helped support their brother tribes, as they settled into the Promised Land. Joshua is advising them to be watchful, to be alert, as they keep the commandment of Moses. Why is this so important?

Throughout life, we tend to grow complacent. When things are going well, we become quite comfortable and often ignore God and His plans. When our selfish plans begin to garner our time and attention, that's when things usually fall apart.

When we're not loving God with all we are and all we have—when we're not in the Word—we're allowing room for the world's vision and values to seep into our heart and soul and begin to take root, crowding out God and His perfect plan for us.

The simple truth is that life centered around God is just better. And who doesn't want to live a better life? Cling to Him today. Make Him your primary focus, and watch the blessings abound. You won't regret it—not even for a minute!

Heavenly Father, with all I am, with all I have. . .I love You! Amen.

BRINGING HIS PEOPLE HOME

*"And what do I see flying like clouds to Israel, like doves
to their nests? They are ships from the ends of the earth,
from lands that trust in me, led by the great ships of Tarshish.
They are bringing the people of Israel home from far away,
carrying their silver and gold. They will honor the LORD your God,
the Holy One of Israel, for he has filled you with splendor."*

ISAIAH 60:8–9 NLT

What an amazing picture, painted thousands of years ago! The Israelites have always longed for their home, Israel. Many times, they have been stranded or enslaved far, far away, but the heart of God for His children is a glorious homegoing.

Maybe you can relate. Maybe you've felt like a child lost in the wilderness, wanting to go home. Today, God is calling you back to Himself. No matter where you are, no matter how far you've wandered, no matter how many times you've convinced yourself that going home isn't an option, He's right there, crying out for you to run into His arms.

Don't wait another minute. Like a dove, fly to your nest and find true rest in Him, once and for all.

*Lord, I want to go home! No more wandering for me. I've been in the
wilderness too long. I've experienced too much. Today I choose to
run back into Your arms, as the Israelites sprinted toward Jerusalem.
There's no place sweeter than being at home with You, Father. Amen.*

ALL I WANT!

You're all I want in heaven! You're all I want on earth!. . .GOD is
rock-firm and faithful. Look! Those who left you are falling apart!
. . . But I'm in the very presence of God—oh, how refreshing it is!
I've made Lord GOD my home. God, I'm telling the world what you do!

PSALM 73:25–28 MSG

There are so many things to enjoy on earth: the beauty of God's creation, fun with family and friends, our favorite foods, travel. . . Yet none compare with the glory of heaven: walls decorated with precious stones, streets of pure gold. . .no mourning, no tears, no pain—only eternal joy! (Read Revelation 21.) However, it *all* pales in comparison to experiencing the presence of God for eternity.

Asaph, the writer of Psalm 73, beautifully expressed a heart of longing—a heart that recognizes *nothing* in heaven or on earth can compare to forever spent in the presence of God. Can the human mind even fathom eternity? Certainly, our finite brains can't even come close!

Woman of God, what does your heart long for today? Do you crave the refreshment of eternity in heaven—*forever* in your heavenly Father's presence? Put your mind on the things of heaven today (Colossians 3:2)!

Lord, my heart longs for eternity with You, and I don't
want to keep it to myself. Who needs to hear the reason
for my hope today? Show me, Father. Amen.

108

LITTLE CHILD

People were also bringing babies to Jesus for him to place his hands on them. When the disciples saw this, they rebuked them. But Jesus called the children to him and said, "Let the little children come to me, and do not hinder them, for the kingdom of God belongs to such as these. Truly I tell you, anyone who will not receive the kingdom of God like a little child will never enter it."
LUKE 18:15–17 NIV

How beautiful are the words of Jesus: "The kingdom of God belongs to such as these"!

The disciples were disgusted that parents were bringing their babies to Jesus. Certainly, Jesus was too important to be bothered with infants! But Jesus' immediate intervention showed He welcomed even the youngest of children. He would turn none away.

These passages from the book of Luke remind us that *all* are welcome in God's Kingdom. Even when we can't fathom His welcome. . .even when it doesn't make sense. . .Jesus says, "Come!" Come and experience joy and wholeness. Come and encounter His love and grace. Approach Him with expectation and excitement. Approach Him as a child, fully dependent upon the one who gave Himself for us.

God, when I sometimes try to reason why some should be welcome in Your presence and why others shouldn't, remind me of Your Word. Remind me of Your salvation made available to all. Help me to approach You as a child, Lord. Amen.

CLIMBING TREES

Jesus [said]. . ."Zacchaeus, come down immediately. I must stay at your house today." So he came down at once and welcomed him gladly. All the people saw this and began to mutter, "He has gone to be the guest of a sinner." But Zacchaeus stood up and said to the Lord, "Look, Lord! Here and now I give half of my possessions to the poor, and if I have cheated anybody out of anything, I will pay back four times the amount."

LUKE 19:5–8 NIV

Zacchaeus probably thought quite highly of himself. He had an important job as a tax collector, but he was hated by many because of his dishonesty. He took more than he was supposed to from the people and pocketed the extra cash for himself.

Despite Zacchaeus' flawed character, he would do *anything*—even climb a tree!—just to get a better view of Jesus. He was willing to face possible public humiliation to get a glimpse of the Lord. He was so moved by Jesus that he was even willing to pay back "four times the amount" he stole in tax money.

You'll likely never have to climb a tree to see Jesus, but what are you willing to do to spend time in His presence? Will you do *whatever* it takes?

Jesus, thank You for showing us how You warmly received the sinner Zacchaeus. . .a beautiful reminder that You'll receive me as well. I love You, Lord. Amen.

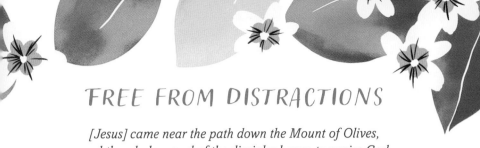

FREE FROM DISTRACTIONS

[Jesus] came near the path down the Mount of Olives,
and the whole crowd of the disciples began to praise God
joyfully with a loud voice for all the miracles they had seen:
The King who comes in the name of the Lord is the blessed
One. Peace in heaven and glory in the highest heaven!
LUKE 19:37–38 HCSB

What occupies your mind throughout the day? Are you able to stay focused on what truly matters? Or do your thoughts dart from worry to worry? Is your heart centered on the Savior—or on the world's distractions?

When Jesus came onto the scene, as described in these verses from the book of Luke, the crowd was wholly focused on Him. They had nothing but Jesus and praise on their minds. Their words and actions showed their honor and love for Jesus. Certainly, the people in the crowd had problems of their own—maybe a sick family member, possibly a difficult relationship, or perhaps tight finances. Regardless, they didn't let their human problems stand in the way of celebrating and praising Jesus. Their focus on the one who matters most kept them free from life's distractions.

Today, keep your heart and mind focused on Jesus. What are you praising Him for today? When your focus is heavenward, your soul will overflow with thanksgiving!

Father God, I praise You for all You have done in my life.
Thank You for saving me, for blessing me. I love You! Amen.

WHO BUT GOD?

Who but God goes up to heaven and comes back down?
Who holds the wind in his fists? Who wraps up the oceans
in his cloak? Who has created the whole wide world?
What is his name—and his son's name? Tell me if you know!

PROVERBS 30:4 NLT

No person has gone to heaven and returned to earth to tell us mortals what they've seen. Sure, Enoch and Elijah were taken into heaven while they were still alive (Genesis 5:24 and 2 Kings 2:11), but heaven is where they stayed. Their tickets to heaven were one-way only. Going up to heaven and coming back down? God is the only one who has this power.

And it's certainly not within the realm of human possibility for any man or woman to set the winds free to blow or to bring them to stillness. The power lies with the heavenly Creator alone, who has complete control over the winds and the seas that obey Him (Psalm 135:7; Matthew 8:26–27).

God—and only God—has the ability to create the entire world and everything in it. All of creation is in His powerful, capable hands. Who but God, indeed?

Lord God, I can go to sleep in peace each night, knowing that You
alone are in control of the entire world and everything in it. Thank You
for calming my heart even as You calm the winds and waves. Amen.

STAY. WAIT. TRUST.

I'm sure now I'll see God's goodness in the
exuberant earth. Stay with GOD! Take heart.
Don't quit. I'll say it again: Stay with GOD.
PSALM 27:13–14 MSG

David had a lot to worry about. He had every reason to be afraid. He was at war with powerful armies, and His enemies were approaching. He was in a stressful position to say the least. No one would have blamed David had he panicked and run for his life. Nor would it have been any surprise had he chosen to run blindly into battle. It's difficult to stay cool, calm, and collected under pressure.

But David had *the one thing* that grounded him—the one thing that could keep him focused and clear-headed. And that one thing was complete trust in the goodness of God. David knew, without a doubt, that waiting on God was the very best solution for a bad situation. Why? Because God has everything under control, and He will always show us the way to go (Deuteronomy 31:8). He will reveal the very best solution to our problems.

When your world is crumbling, no matter how bad things get, take heart! Stay. Wait. Trust. God has it all in His hands.

Heavenly Father, sometimes life is hard and scary,
and I can't face it alone. I need You! And so, I will
stay. I will wait. I will trust You, Lord. Amen.

MORNING JOY

Sing the praises of the Lord, you his faithful people;
praise his holy name. For his anger lasts only a moment,
but his favor lasts a lifetime; weeping may stay for
the night, but rejoicing comes in the morning.
PSALM 30:4–5 NIV

During our hardest trials, the nights are long. When we toss and turn and can't sleep. . . When we can't stop the tears from falling. . . When our minds race with negative thoughts. . . When we don't have the words or even the energy to pray. . . When it seems like our world will never be made right again. . . There is hope because God's Word promises that morning will come! And with the new morning comes hope! And hope will always come because of Jesus.

Although we may not have a smooth and easy road ahead, our loving heavenly Father is beside us every step of the way. And, if we stick close to Him, He offers us His favor. He promises that joy will come again despite the pain and sorrow we're experiencing in the moment.

So, like the psalmist, offer your sincerest praise. Thank the heavenly Father for His love. Thank Him for His promises. Thank Him for new mornings of rejoicing after long, sleepless nights.

Lord, thank You for Your favor. You are so good to
me. Although You don't promise me a life free from
hardship and pain, You do promise hope and joy.

HANDPICKED

God the Father knew you and chose you long ago, and his Spirit has made you holy. As a result, you have obeyed him and have been cleansed by the blood of Jesus Christ.

1 PETER 1:2 NLT

No matter how beautiful, accomplished, athletic, smart, capable, creative, or loving we might be, we've all experienced rejection: didn't get the job; didn't make the team; didn't receive the scholarship; didn't get asked to the dance; didn't get the leadership appointment; didn't get a second date; got cheated on; never received an invitation; didn't make first chair.

Try as we might to pretend we don't care when we're not chosen, rejection hurts. A lot. Young or old, green or experienced, simple or sophisticated, rejection makes us question our worth and wonder why we even try.

Before Jesus came, only the nation of Israel could claim to be God's chosen people. But because of Christ, all believers—Jews and Gentiles—belong to God. Here's a beautiful truth in scripture, sister: When you were born, God had already chosen and accepted you. Your salvation and security rest in the free and merciful choice of your almighty God, and nothing can take away His love for those who believe in Him (Romans 8:38–39).

Father, You chose me first, but I choose You now and forever. Thank You for wanting me even if others reject me. You hold my heart, God. I trust You with it. Amen.

115

WONDERS OF HIS LOVE

*Praise be to the LORD, for he showed me the wonders of
his love when I was in a city under siege. In my alarm
I said, "I am cut off from your sight!" Yet you heard
my cry for mercy when I called to you for help.*

Dictionary.com defines *wonder* as: "something strange and surprising; a cause of surprise, astonishment, or admiration." Here in Psalm 31, David was praising God because God had shown him the *wonders* of His love. David was awestruck with the unexpected love His heavenly Father had shown to him—especially during challenging times.

It's difficult to comprehend the overwhelming, unchanging, never-ending love of God with our finite human brains. After all, we're conditioned to expect love with limits. Human love is conditional after all. It's imperfect. It's inconsistent. It fails more often than we'd like to admit. But God's love is big. It's generous. It never changes. It runs so deep that it's hard for us to fathom. God's love is quite astonishing!

When you find yourself disappointed by love—the love of a friend, family member, or fellow church-goer—think on Psalm 31. Remember, there is one who loves you without limits. Praise Him!

*Lord of love, I praise You! Although I can't fully comprehend the
depths to which You love me, I am so grateful. When human love fails,
remind me to look to You—the one who loves me fully and without limits.*

THE HOPEFUL WAIT

We wait in hope for the LORD; he is our help and our shield.
In him our hearts rejoice, for we trust in his holy name. May your
unfailing love be with us, LORD, even as we put our hope in you.

PSALM 33:20–22 NIV

So often our waiting times are full of stress and anxiety. We wait and worry. . .we worry and wait. And the waiting is made even more difficult when our minds are overflowing with irritating, anxiety-inducing "what if" thoughts like:

What if I lose my job?
What if my friend won't forgive me?
What if I end up alone?
What if my future doesn't go as planned?

Waiting doesn't often feel hopeful, does it? . . . Is there even such a thing as "hopeful waiting"? The answer, according to God's Word, is *yes*!

Whatever you're waiting for, God is a constant hope. You can trust Him because He's got everything under control. He sees all. He hears all. He knows all. And if that's not enough to ease your worried mind, He is our shield of protection. . .and His love is unfailing!

So, dear one, rejoice! Receive His protection. Welcome His love. In the most difficult waiting season, He will come to your rescue!

Father God, I will take heart as I wait. Thank You for
rescuing me, even in the most difficult seasons of life.
I will put my hope and trust in You alone!

117

GOD ONLY KNOWS

[Only] with [God] are [perfect] wisdom and might; He [alone]
has [true] counsel and understanding. Behold, He tears down,
and it cannot be built again. . . . He withholds the waters, and the
land dries up; again, He sends forth [rains], and they overwhelm
the land or transform it. With Him are might and wisdom; the
deceived and the deceiver are His [and in His power].

JOB 12:13–16 AMPC

Some days you may have a million questions as to why God has allowed certain things to happen. Why does He withhold the rains, then later pour them out in a flood that transforms the land? Why does He allow good people to die too soon and the seemingly not-so-good people to live into their nineties?

Instead of getting caught up in trying to figure out the whys of God, trust that He knows best. Eckhart Tolle says, "Sometimes surrender means giving up trying to understand and becoming comfortable with not knowing."

God alone has perfect wisdom and might. He's in total control, knows what He's doing, and has a plan for His people—including you. So no matter what happens, relax. Everything in this world is under God's power. You need not understand everything—but God does. And that's all you need to know.

Sometimes, Lord, I have trouble accepting certain things. Help me to
surrender to Your wisdom and might, to acknowledge the idea that I
don't have to understand everything. But simply trust You for everything.

SO SEND I YOU

Again Jesus said, "Peace be with you! As the
Father has sent me, I am sending you."

JOHN 20:21 NIV

So many great men and women have been nudged from the nest—to serve their countries, to run for political office, to pastor churches, to serve as missionaries, to adopt or foster children, to work in social services, to wear the badge, to pick up the fire hose. All over this globe, people are responding to various calls on their lives, saying, "Here am I, Lord. Send me!"

What does it mean, to receive a call from God? Will you hear an audible voice, as Isaiah did when God's presence filled the temple, or will there be a gentle whisper from the Holy Spirit, prompting you to step out of your comfort zone? Only the Lord knows! But when He has a task for you (and He will), you've got to be ready to jump and run! A battle cry will ring out, a trumpet will sound, or a whisper will tickle your ear, signaling you to the front lines. There's no time to waste, so learn all you can now, while you're waiting.

Here am I, Lord. . .send me! I don't know where. I don't know
when. I don't know how. But I submit myself to the process,
Lord. I want to be usable, pliable, ready to respond when You
sound the cry. Begin to prepare my heart, even now. Amen.

FULLY CONTENTED—
HEART, MIND, AND SOUL

Open your mouth and taste, open your eyes and see—
how good GOD is. Blessed are you who run to him. Worship GOD
if you want the best; worship opens doors to all his goodness.
PSALM 34:8–9 MSG

When you get a "taste" of what the world has to offer, it always leaves you hungry for more. More money. More stuff. More "likes" on social media. Just *more*. Add all the "mores" of the world together, and you'll still end up with a negative number when it comes to contentment! Strangely enough, the world *never* satisfies today—and it never will.

But thankfully, there's one thing that always leads to true contentment—it's the never-ending goodness of God. He's *way* better than anything the world has to offer. And He offers blessings too many to count. He freely gives of His love, His kindness, His rescue, and He offers eternal life (if we only say yes to His gift of salvation).

Each of God's many blessings leads to real, lasting contentment. It's true! Just take a taste and see for yourself. You'll never long for a taste of the world again! Your heart, your soul, your mind will be fully satisfied—and that's a promise you can count on!

God, thank You for providing all I need to experience true
contentment here on earth. You are so much better than anything
the world offers. You are my everything. You're all I need.

A LOSS FOR WORDS

But he most surely did listen, he came on the double
when he heard my prayer. Blessed be God: he didn't
turn a deaf ear, he stayed with me, loyal in his love.

PSALM 66:19–20 MSG

There may be some seasons in life when God seems to be speaking directly to you every moment. Because of that close connection with Him, you're filled with confidence and the assurance of His presence. Yet there may be some seasons when God seems completely and utterly silent—and you may start to question whether He's even listening, leading you into areas of uncertainty and doubt.

Be assured that God does listen. To every prayer, every cry, every praise. When you can't find the words, He takes in the groans of your heart.

Your God is "loyal in his love." He is with you even when the world around you seems to be crumbling. God's with you even when you sin and fall short. God's with You even when He appears to be silent.

God has promised to never leave you (Deuteronomy 31:6). So place your trust in Him continually. Then you'll have a firm foundation to stand on when life starts quaking. Even if you can't find the words, spend time in His presence. He'll stay with you as long as you need.

God, thank You for always being there, for always listening, for always
being loyal in Your love. With You in my life, nothing can shake me.

THE BETTER THING

When Jesus was. . .a guest of Simon the Leper, a woman. . .anointed him with a bottle of very expensive perfume. . . . The disciples. . .were furious. . . . [Jesus] intervened. "Why are you giving this woman a hard time? She has just done something wonderfully significant for me. . . . When she poured this perfume on my body, what she really did was anoint me for burial. You can be sure that. . .what she has just done is going to be remembered and admired."

MATTHEW 26:6–13 MSG

The woman mentioned in Matthew 26 anointed Jesus with a jar of very pricey perfume. The disciples immediately criticized her for her actions; but rather than remaining silent or nodding in agreement, Jesus came to her defense.

Where the disciples saw only waste, Jesus saw significance. Beyond the pouring out of the perfume, He saw a beautiful act of love worthy of being remembered. And He said so!

How do you want to be remembered? As a successful career woman? A fabulous cook? A wonderful wife and mother? While nothing is wrong with these things, perhaps the better thing would be to be remembered for our love. When we do everything in love, the Lord will take notice. He'll speak up in our favor!

When I am criticized for any action that comes from a place of love, Father, I am so thankful You always have my back.

OPENING THE GATES

*Open for me the gates where the righteous enter, and I will go in and thank the L*ORD. *These gates lead to the presence of the L*ORD, *and the godly enter there. . . . This is the day the L*ORD *has made. We will rejoice and be glad in it. . . . The L*ORD *is God, shining upon us.*
PSALM 118:19–20, 24, 27 NLT

No transformation can take place unless you're in sync with God, walking in step with Him, following His every prompt, nudge, whisper. That requires you lowering your resistance to God and His will. Trusting Him enough with yourself, your loved ones, your present and future, everything you have and are, and walking through the gates that lead to God's presence.

Today, consider areas in your life in which you may not be giving God full sway. Where are you feeling resistance to His message, hints, and commands? What things or people have you not turned over to Him, surrendered to His gentle care and touch? Which worries are leading you to places of doubt and fear?

Ask God to open your eyes to concerns that are best left in His care. Then surrender them to Him as you walk through the gates that lead to His presence. And rejoice, for God has made this day for you.

Lord, reveal, then tear down any barrier that exists between me and Thee. For I long to enter Your gates with praise upon my lips.

STEADFAST

How precious is your steadfast love, O God! The children of mankind take refuge in the shadow of your wings. They feast on the abundance of your house, and you give them drink from the river of your delights. For with you is the fountain of life.

PSALM 36:7–9 ESV

God's love is steadfast—it's constant and unmoving, firmly fixed in place. A steadfast love won't fade. It won't change. It won't fail.

These verses from Psalm 36 celebrate all the blessings Christ-followers receive because of God's steadfast love: gifts of His protection, His provision, His life, His light. When we accept Christ into our hearts and make Him Lord of our lives, we enter a relationship with Him. And when we walk closely with Him, our life is like a continual feast where only the best food and drink are offered. Where we're always satisfied. Always safe. Where we never lack a single thing.

If you've accepted Christ as your Lord and Savior, enjoy the feast! If you haven't, take the step toward a fulfilling life today. Pray this prayer right now:

Heavenly Father, thank You for Your steadfast love. I claim all the blessings a life with You has to offer. Please forgive my sins. Thank You for sending Jesus to take my punishment—the punishment I deserved. I accept Your gift of eternal life. I want to change my life starting right now. I want to walk with You all my days.

GOD'S PLAN

For in You, O Lord, do I hope; You will answer, O Lord my God.
PSALM 38:15 AMPC

Say the words of this psalm out loud. Do you have this kind of unwavering hope? Do you *really* believe God hears and will answer?

If you've ever put your hope in a human relationship, odds are you were let down at some point. You were disappointed by a broken promise. Or things just didn't go quite like you had planned. The problem is that, just as in our human relationships, we often put our very limited human expectations on God. And then, when He does things His way (and not ours), we feel let down. We're disappointed. *We had a plan, after all, and God didn't stick to it!*

The difference is that humans are imperfect. They're selfish. And they don't always look out for our well-being. But we can trust that when God doesn't do things our way, it's for good reason. Because He knows what's truly best for us. So, we can always hope in His plan. We can wholeheartedly trust that He will answer at the right time. And whatever His plan, it's perfect!

"For I know the plans I have for you," says the LORD.
"They are plans for good. . .to give you a future and a hope."
JEREMIAH 29:11 NLT

God, I'm sorry for all the times I've put my limited human expectations on You. You are my hope, and I trust You!

WATCHING OVER

*The LORD watches over the foreigner and sustains the fatherless
and the widow, but he frustrates the ways of the wicked.*

PSALM 146:9 NIV

Lost. Abandoned. Neglected. Forgotten. There are times in each of our lives when we may have these feelings. And we don't have to be a refugee or an orphan or have lost a spouse to feel lonely. But because we do feel these ways, we should be able to imagine all the more what it must be like to be in a position in which you have suddenly lost everything that makes home feel like home and all the things that are familiar and bring comfort. And we should then be able to have compassion for those who are in such a position.

Yet our gentle, loving, ever-present Father God transforms us. He watches over us and cares for us and provides for us. In His love, we are changed—those who are lost are found. Those who are fatherless are welcomed into Daddy's arms. Those with broken hearts are made whole again. God's love is powerful and surprising—showing up in some of the most mysterious places. And every time we are met with unconditional love, with unmerited favor, with generous gifts of grace, we can know that we are experiencing the love of our perfect Father.

Lord, thank You for Your gentle love that makes me Your child. Amen.

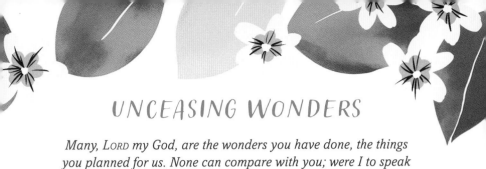

UNCEASING WONDERS

Many, LORD my God, are the wonders you have done, the things you planned for us. None can compare with you; were I to speak and tell of your deeds, they would be too many to declare.

PSALM 40:5 NIV

Think about all the amazing people you know and the wonderful impact they've had on the world. Certainly, you know women who have selflessly cared for the sick and dying. You probably know a handful of men and women who have donated thousands of dollars to charity. Perhaps you're acquainted with someone whose invention has improved the world. All are fantastic contributions, for sure. . .but when you think of the wonders of God, can anything really compare?

The honest answer is no—because there is no end to His wonders. Creation. Miracles. Salvation. Blessings. His love. His grace. His glory. His omnipotence. His omniscience. His power. His compassion. It's not even possible to name them all, because His wonders continue, even now! But sadly, our human tendency is to *ooh* and *aah* over the accomplishments and generosity of men and women, while we often overlook the limitless love and power of our heavenly Father.

Take a moment right now to increase your joy by thinking on the wonders of our God. And then spend time in quiet conversation with the one who loves you most.

God of unceasing wonders, forgive me for all the times I've failed to recognize Your greatness. Nothing compares to You!

MARVELOUS LOVE

What marvelous love the Father has extended to us!
Just look at it—we're called children of God!

1 JOHN 3:1 MSG

Our world, our culture can become so loud, you may seek a quiet place of peace to escape the noise. As God's child, within you His marvelous love rests, providing a refuge in quiet times with Him.

Think about the cradle songs that soothe small children when they are nervous, distraught, or fearful. As you sing softly, their tears diminish and a stillness comes over them. Much like a baby's lullaby, God's love can silence worry, confusion, fear, and anxiety. His gentle and abiding love flows through you, reminding you that He alone holds the world in His hands.

Charles Finney shared an experience he had of God's amazing love. "The Holy Spirit descended upon me in a manner that seemed to go through me, body and soul. I could feel the impression like a wave of electricity going through and through me. Indeed, it seemed to come in waves and waves of liquid love. . .like the very breath of God. . .it seemed to fan me like immense wings."

Allow God to bring sanctuary to your heart as you take a moment of quiet, resting in His miraculous love.

God, pour Your love out on me as I take in these
quiet moments in Your presence today.

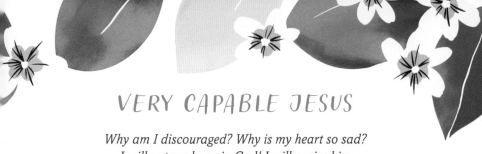

VERY CAPABLE JESUS

Why am I discouraged? Why is my heart so sad?
I will put my hope in God! I will praise him
again—my Savior and my God!
PSALM 42:5–6 NLT

Anger. Sadness. Depression. Anxiety. Hopelessness. Despair. All are running rampant in our world today. Ask anyone, and it seems the consensus is: life is hard, and it's getting harder by the minute. Fewer people are capable of coping with the stress of it all. They can't do it alone. They need help. They need hope. *They need Jesus.*

God never promised life would be easy (see John 16:33). The Christian life doesn't come with a magic wand that protects us from all things horrible or hard. There's no hocus-pocus prayer to eradicate the world's problems. Life is sometimes difficult, and there's no way around it.

But, dear one, there is hope! Because when we accept Jesus as the Lord of our lives, what we *do* have is a very capable Jesus. When we *can't*, He *can*! The Bible is overflowing with promises of His power, His love, His salvation, His faithfulness. Hope in Jesus today. The future looks bright when your gaze is fixed on Him!

I am discouraged and depressed. I need Your help coping,
Father. I can't do it on my own. You are big enough to handle
all my problems and the world's problems too. And so, I will
place every worry and fear in Your perfectly capable hands.

KEEP ME SAFE

I did nothing to deserve this, GOD, crossed no one, wronged no one.
All the same, they're after me, determined to get me. Wake up and
see for yourself! You're GOD, GOD-of-Angel-Armies, Israel's God!

PSALM 59:4 MSG

When Saul is removed from the kingship by God through Samuel, and David is elevated, Saul is bewildered about why he is deposed. It is impossibly hard for him to accept the reign of David. So, he sends henchmen after David.

David prays to the Lord to keep him safe from the jealous attacks of Saul. David knows both that he has not done anything wrong (this time) and that Saul too is anointed by God. David only wants God to shield him from misguided attacks. Though he is in power, he asks the God he loves for protection.

The assaults you may face will probably never rise to the seriousness of the ones David faced. Yet you may be inundated by all sorts of cares and pressures, stresses and worries that certainly drive you to the wall. Then it is that you find yourself realizing the extent of your weakness and turning quickly to God for strength. And the God who commands the armies of angels is somehow, astoundingly, merciful to you.

Dear Lord, in my weakness let me rely on Your strength. Protect me from the cares that assault me needlessly; soothe away my worries. Amen.

CONFUSION TO CONFIDENCE

Why do You sleep, O Lord? Arouse Yourself, cast us not off forever! Why do You hide Your face and forget our affliction and our oppression? For our lives are bowed down to the dust. . . . Come to our help, and deliver us for Your mercy's sake and because of Your steadfast love!

PSALM 44:23–26 AMPC

Have you ever witnessed wonderful Christian people experience unbearable, undeserved pain and suffering? It's confusing and unfair, isn't it? Such was the feeling of the Israelites whose relationship with God was based on His promise that if they followed His instruction, they'd be blessed. But their enemies were winning—and it seemed like God had turned His back and left them defenseless.

According to the psalmist, Israel had done nothing wrong: they had not strayed from God, nor had they been unfaithful to Him (see verses 17 and 18). Despite their confusion, the Israelites still believed God would act on their behalf. They knew that, no matter what, His love was unfailing. The Israelites could have turned sour on God. They could have said, "Looks like we're on our own!" But they *knew* God. They trusted Him.

And so should we. When it seems like God is far away, tell Him you need Him. Tell Him you are confident in His protection and love. Then wait for Him to show up. Because He will!

God, I need You. Though I am confused, I trust You will show up!

PEACE LIKE A RIVER

"I have told you these things, so that in me you may
have peace. In this world you will have trouble.
But take heart! I have overcome the world."
JOHN 16:33 NIV

It was starting out to be a rotten day. Beth overslept and got a speeding ticket on the way to work. Upon arriving, she found that the receptionist had called in sick and the other assistant was on bereavement leave. Beth was responsible to cover everything in her small office. The sales team didn't seem to understand why she couldn't keep up with their rapid-fire requests. On the brink of tears, Beth felt overwhelmed and discouraged.

Life often feels like a stormy sea instead of a calm, peaceful river. Circumstances have the capacity to upend us, making us feel unstable and out of control. True, flowing peace comes from Jesus. It is in Jesus that we can have confidence and a mind that is calm, tranquil, and unmoved. The events of life can cause us to take our eyes off Jesus. Our river of peace lies in our Savior.

Gracious and loving Father, we thank You for Your peace, the
peace that surpasses all understanding. When circumstances
cause me to take my eyes off You, please remind me that You
are my peace, my confidence, and my joy. Circumstances can
change. You never do! Thank You for loving me so. Amen.

CENTER TRUTH

Praise the Lord. . . . For great is His love toward us, and the faithfulness of the Lord endures forever. Praise the Lord.

PSALM 117:1–2 NIV

Consisting of only two verses, Psalm 117 is the central chapter of the Bible. The awesome, sovereign God arranged that His Words be handed to twenty-first-century believers with these truths at their heart:

Praise the Lord. Exalt Him.

Whoever, wherever you are.

Great is His love toward you.

His faithfulness endures forever.

The Westminster Catechism asks and answers, "What is the chief end of man? *To glorify God and enjoy Him forever"* (emphasis added).

Praise God for His great love that created humankind and gave His only begotten Son so people might have eternal life. His love does not change and never fails.

Praise God for His eternal faithfulness. He always has been and always will be faithful. What He says, He'll do. Who He is doesn't change (see Hebrews 13:8).

King Hezekiah trusted the eternal God. When Sennacherib's army surrounded Jerusalem, Hezekiah told his people, "There is a greater power with us than with him" (2 Chronicles 32:7 NIV).

Whatever's going on in your life today, pause to praise the Lord. The God who rescued Hezekiah, who loves you and is faithful forever, is with you today.

Eternal God, today and always let me glorify and trust You.

TAPPING INTO POWER

She. . .touched his robe. For she thought to herself, "If I can just touch his robe, I will be healed." Immediately the bleeding stopped. . . . Jesus realized at once that healing power had gone out from him.
MARK 5:27–30 NLT

A nameless woman with an issue of blood had gone to so many doctors, trying to be healed of her internal hemorrhaging. She'd spent everything she had for a cure but instead of getting better, she grew worse. Then she heard about Jesus.

One in a crowd of many, the woman came up behind Jesus. As she reached out to touch Him, she thought, "If I can just touch his robe, I will be healed." That silent prayer of faith enabled her to tap into the power of a living God. And she became whole once more.

Knowing His power had been released, Jesus stopped. He asked who'd touched Him. Trembling, the woman came before Him, fell at His feet, and confessed it had been her. His verbal response was as potent as His physical release of power as He put words to her experience, saying, "Daughter, your faith has made you well" (Mark 5:34 NLT).

When you need help, take up your mantle of trust, extend your hand, and make a connection with Jesus. And you too will be able to tap into His power.

I reach out to You in this moment, Jesus, my faith in hand. Amen.

NO FLOWERY WORDS

I'm standing my ground, GOD, shouting for help, at my prayers every morning, on my knees each daybreak. Why, GOD, do you turn a deaf ear? Why do you make yourself scarce? For as long as I remember I've been hurting; I've taken the worst you can hand out, and I've had it. Your wildfire anger has blazed through my life; I'm bleeding, black-and-blue. You've attacked me fiercely from every side, raining down blows till I'm nearly dead.
PSALM 88:13–18 MSG

The writer of this psalm is in deep despair. He holds nothing back in his communication to God. He doesn't use flowery words. He doesn't make light of his situation. In fact, he's talking tough—he's standing his ground with God. And he means business!

So often we take the soft approach with God. Christians are supposed to be sweet, gentle and soft-spoken. . .right? And sometimes, that flows into our relationship with God. We forget that we can be 100 percent real with Him, 100 percent of the time. So, we hold back our feelings in our prayers. But God is big enough to handle whatever we lay on Him. Our anger. Our fears. Our worries. Our disappointments. Our hurts. He can take it! He only cares that we bring it *all* to Him. Because that's where our troubled hearts should go—directly to our heavenly Father.

*God, I have no flowery words to share with You today.
I am hurting. I need You now! Please help me!*

I GIVE UP

God so loved the world that he gave his one and only Son,
that whoever believes in him shall not perish but have eternal life.
JOHN 3:16 NIV

God encourages us to surrender to Him. How does God expect us to do that? *Merriam-Webster* defines *surrender* as "to give (oneself) over to something (as an influence)." God has given us free will, so the choice becomes ours: to surrender or maintain total control.

When we make the decision to surrender, we give ourselves over to God and allow His authority in our lives. We place our hope in the God who runs the universe. Oswald Chambers said, "The choice is either to say, 'I will not surrender,' or to surrender, breaking the hard shell of individuality, which allows the spiritual life to emerge."

Isn't that an amazing thought? Our Creator God cares enough about us to delve into our everyday lives and help us. Through the Holy Spirit within, God's gentle hand of direction will sustain each of us, enabling us to grow closer to our Father. The closer we grow, the more like Him we desire to be. Then His influence spreads through us to others. When we surrender, He is able to use our lives and enrich others. What a powerful message: give up and give more!

Lord, thank You for loving us despite our frailties.
What an encouragement to me today. Amen.

KNOWN BY LOVE

[Dear] little children. . .you are not able to come where
I am going. I give you a new commandment: . . . Just as
I have loved you, so you too should love one another.
By this shall all [men] know that you are My disciples.

JOHN 13:33–35 AMPC

After Jesus explains to His disciples that they can't go with Him to the cross, He gives them a new commandment: "Just as I have loved you, so you too should love one another." He had already told the Jews they should love each other, but this "new" commandment came with a higher standard: to love *as He loves*. Jesus assures the disciples this is how all people will know they are His true followers. Their love will be what sets them apart from the rest of the world.

You might be thinking, *How is it possible to love like Jesus? Christ's love is a divine, unconditional love. . .and human love has limits*. There is truth to this. While humans, left to their own devices, *can't* love like Jesus; humans *with Jesus can love like Jesus*. He makes all things possible, including our ability to love like Him! (See Matthew 19:26; Luke 1:37; Philippians 4:13; Mark 10:27.)

Today, set a new, higher standard for yourself as you show others the love of Christ. Ask God for His help!

God, I want to be known by my love—a love that looks like Yours!

GOD IS IN THIS PLACE

When Jacob awoke from his sleep, he thought, "Surely the
LORD is in this place, and I was not aware of it." He was
afraid and said, "How awesome is this place! This is none
other than the house of God; this is the gate of heaven."
GENESIS 28:16–17 NIV

While journeying back to his grandfather's homeland, Jacob grew weary and laid down under the stars to sleep. An amazing dream followed. He saw a great stairway reaching up to the heavens. God's angels were going up and down the stairway. In the dream, the Lord stood right beside Jacob. He said, "Your descendants will be like the dust of the earth, and you will spread out to the west and the east, to the north and the south. All peoples on earth will be blessed through you and your offspring" (Genesis 28:14 NIV).

Jacob awoke from the dream, overcome by the promise he'd received in his sleep. Instead of simply moving on, he paused to acknowledge the place where the dream had taken place. He called the place Bethel.

Do you stop to acknowledge God when He speaks into your life? Can you think back to your "Bethel" moments? When and where did God speak to your heart and give you the courage to go on? Today, thank Him for His many Bethel encounters.

Thank You, Lord, for my Bethel encounters! May I never
forget those times when You've spoken to my heart. Amen.

A JIGSAW PUZZLE LIFE

*GOD made my life complete when I placed all the pieces before him. . . .
He gave me a fresh start. . . . I haven't taken God for granted.
Every day I review the ways he works. . . . I feel put back together.*
2 SAMUEL 22:21–25 MSG

Sometimes life feels like a giant jigsaw puzzle with lots of teeny-tiny pieces—and many of them have gone missing.

David knew what a "missing puzzle pieces" life was like. He experienced it firsthand. But instead of lamenting and keeping his focus on how bad things were, he chose to turn everything over to God. He gave God His whole life—every single puzzle piece—and submitted to Him. David, though imperfect, lived for God. He kept God's rules and fully depended on God. And though he sometimes failed, David never turned away from Him. And so, God rewarded David for his righteousness. He took the pieces of David's life and put it all back together.

Like David, we too can make the wise choice to give our puzzle pieces to God. When we ask for help, God hears. He will put the puzzle of our lives back together, creating a complete and beautiful picture of beauty, hope, and faith.

*Father God, my life sometimes feels like a jumbled mess,
and I need Your help! Today, I give all the pieces of
my life to You. I trust You to put it all together.*

IN HIS HANDS

Jesus answered them, "Do you finally believe? In fact,
you're about to make a run for it—saving your own skins and
abandoning me. But. . . The Father is with me. I've told you
all this so that. . .you will be unshakable and assured, deeply
at peace. In this godless world you will continue to experience
difficulties. But take heart! I've conquered the world."

JOHN 16:33 MSG

As Christ-followers, it's easy to become discouraged in a world that seems to move farther and farther away from Jesus. The gap becomes more pronounced by the day. Wars. Disease. Natural disasters. Political unrest. It seems there's one crisis after another. And even those who follow Christ could be pulled into the fray if our focus is too much on the world and not enough on Jesus. Our anxiety and depression may threaten to spiral out of control. We may even lose hope.

But just as God didn't abandon His Son on the cross, Jesus assured His disciples that He was still in control and always would be—because He conquered the world! So, take heart, dear one. As bad as things might seem, our heavenly Father has us in His hands—today, tomorrow, and for eternity! With the unfailing promise of Jesus, we have lasting joy, peace, comfort, and hope!

Lord, because of Your unfailing promises, I always have
hope. As the world grows apart from You, draw me closer
to Your heart. Thank You for Your love and salvation!

FAITH-FILLED IMAGINATION

*Truly my soul silently waits for God; from Him comes
my salvation. He only is my rock and my salvation;
He is my defense; I shall not be greatly moved.*
PSALM 62:1–2 NKJV

Whether it's nagging daytime fears or Technicolor nightmares, worry is something all of us know. We're made to be creative thinkers, but all of us have wished now and then that our imaginations would just *slow down*. God knows the power of imagination, which may be why He gave us so many concrete pictures about Himself in scripture for us to hold on to. The psalms are full of this imagery: God is a "rock," a "strong tower;" He even has "wings" to cover us as a mother hen does her chicks (Psalm 62:2, Psalm 61:3, Psalm 91:4). A vivid image of God's strength and safety can help in the moments our worries overwhelm.

You can also pick a physical "touchstone" to remind you of God's character. One man kept a rock on his desk to signal the safety and solidity of his heavenly Father. One author thanked God for His goodness every time she saw wild doves—reminders of God's Holy Spirit's continual presence—from her window. What touchstone could you use to turn your imagination to God's attributes on your worry-filled days?

*Father, thank You for the gift of imagination and
creativity. When I feel worried, help me dwell on things
that remind me of Your goodness and care for me.*

141

TAKE COVER

Those who live in the shelter of the Most High will find rest in the shadow of the Almighty. . . . He alone is my refuge, my place of safety. . . . He will rescue you. . .and protect you. . . . He will cover you with his feathers. He will shelter you with his wings.

PSALM 91:1–4 NLT

Imagine a helpless baby bird snuggled up safe and cozy in the warm, fluffy feathers of his mama. There, under her wings, he is protected, cared for, sheltered from the dangers of the outside world. In the nest, mama bird will shield her baby from the storms and deliver daily meals to keep him healthy and growing stronger every day.

This is a beautiful picture of how the heavenly Father cares for us. There will always be danger in the world. There will be troubles and worries that plague our minds and pain our hearts. Yet, when we know Jesus, we live in the "shelter of the Most High." And there, we are safe and secure. He will cover us and rescue us from the hard things. . .and in the safety of His presence, we can truly rest and find comfort for our weary souls.

When you find yourself in need of rescue, run to Him! Take cover under His wings of protection and love!

My refuge, my God, thank You for being my safe place.
In You, I take comfort. In You, I find sweet rest.

YOUR FAVORITE "GO-TO"

The Lord says, "I will rescue those who love me. I will protect those who trust in my name. When they call on me, I will answer; I will be with them in trouble. . .rescue and honor them. I will reward them with a long life and give them my salvation."

<small>PSALM 91:14–16 NLT</small>

Who do you call when you need advice? Who listens when you need to talk? Who has your back, lending unwavering support or a helping hand when you need it most? Surely there's one person who is your go-to, most trusted human being of all time.

But has your "go-to" person ever broken a promise? Left your urgent text unopened or unanswered, your important call unreturned? Humans, even the very best of them, let us down sometimes.

But there is one who can be trusted every second, every minute, every hour of every day of every year. His name is Jesus. And when we trust Him wholly, when we love Him completely, He makes good on all His promises and—even better!—He offers us many wonderful things in return. He assures us of His presence. His rescue. His honor. His reward. His salvation.

Have you chosen to follow Jesus? If you have, praise Him! If you haven't, it's not too late!

My Lord and Savior, I trust You. I love You. Come into my heart. I want to follow You, praise and honor You all my days.

CELEBRATE!

*It is a good and delightful thing to give thanks to the Lord,
to sing praises. . .to Your name, O Most High, to show forth
Your loving-kindness in the morning and Your faithfulness
by night. . . . For You, O Lord, have made me glad by Your
works; at the deeds of Your hands I joyfully sing.*

PSALM 92:1–2, 4 AMPC

Some people record their blessings. They keep a journal where they write down the good things that happen every day. This helps them maintain a positive outlook on life and serves as a great reminder that the bad days really aren't *all* bad. There is good in every bad day too!

Here, in Psalm 92, something good has happened, and the psalmist is celebrating and showing his delight in song: "You, O Lord, have made me glad by Your works; at the deeds of Your hands I joyfully sing." Journaling your blessings or singing about them—either way, both are wonderful expressions of the heavenly Father's goodness in everyday living.

This world, while often difficult, doesn't have to leave us down and depressed. When we belong to Jesus, we have the promise of His blessing. We have the benefit of His kindness and goodness. And if we keep our focus on those things, our emotional wellness will benefit mightily. Praise Him!

God, You are so, so good. Help me to keep my focus on Your loving-kindness. Thank You for these wonderful things that happened today.

WHEN DOUBT CREEPS IN

Thomas [said], "Unless I see in his hands the mark of the nails, and place my finger into the mark of the nails, and place my hand into his side, I will never believe."
Eight days later. . .Jesus. . .said to Thomas, "Put your finger here, and see my hands; and put out your hand, and place it in my side. . . ." Thomas answered him, "My Lord and my God!"
JOHN 20:24–28 ESV

If you've ever experienced feelings of doubt when it comes to God, you're in good company. The Bible shares numerous true stories of doubters who needed an extra boost of faith, including:

- Thomas, who doubted Jesus had risen from the dead (verse 25).
- A desperate father, whose son was possessed by an evil spirit (Mark 9:24).
- Sarah, who laughed when God promised to give her a son in her old age (Genesis 18:11–12).

While we know (in our minds) that we can trust God, we often feel (in our hearts) that He might not come through for us. When doubt creeps in and begins to take root, tell God that you're struggling. Be honest. This makes room for Him to step in and meet your need. Then, spend time in His Word. Immersing your heart and mind in God's beautiful, unchanging truth is one of the best ways to free your spirit from doubt. Never forget that *all things are possible* with God (Matthew 19:26)!

Lord, I believe!

MAKING ALLOWANCES

Always be humble and gentle. Be patient with each other,
making allowance for each other's faults because of your love.
EPHESIANS 4:2 NLT

This verse contains such a simple, forgotten truth, doesn't it? God wants us to be holy. He wants us to be righteous and good and godly. But He knows we'll never get it exactly right until we're made perfect in His presence.

Until then, we all have our faults. Numerous faults, if we're honest with ourselves. And God doesn't want us standing around, whispering and pointing self-righteous fingers of condemnation. God is the *only* one who is allowed to wear the judge's robe.

And He doesn't condemn us. Instead, He pours His love and acceptance into our lives, with a gentle admonition to "go and sin no more" (John 8:11 NLT). In other words, "It's okay. You messed up, but it's been taken care of. The price has been paid. I still love you. Just try not to do it again."

Why do we find it so hard to extend grace to others when so much grace has been shown to us? As we go through each day, let's make it a point to live out this verse. Let's be humble, gentle, and patient, making allowances for the faults of others because of God's love.

Dear Father, help me to be gentle and loving with others.
Remind me of the grace You've shown me, and help me
show the same love to those around me. Amen.

SOUL SOOTHER

Who will protect me from the wicked? Who will stand up for me
against evildoers? Unless the LORD had helped me, I would soon
have settled in the silence of the grave. I cried out, "I am slipping!"
but your unfailing love, O LORD, supported me. When doubts filled
my mind, your comfort gave me renewed hope and cheer.

PSALM 94:16–19 NLT

What stresses you out? What doubts seep into your heart and fester? This world is full of hard things that add layers of anxiety to our already-lives. If you were to make a list, you'd probably need an extra-large sheet of paper with line. . .*after line*. . .*after line* of writing space.

When you experience stress and doubt, what calms your anxiety-filled heart? Quiet time with tea and a good book, perhaps? Lunch and conversation with a lifetime bestie? An after-dinner power nap? A warm bubble bath? Certainly, these feel-good things can offer a temporary reprieve from life's chaos. And yet. . .there is something—*someone*—better. This someone offers a lasting, permanent hope for your doubting heart and calm for your anxiety-ridden soul. This someone is the one and only true soul-soother, Jesus.

The writer of Psalm 94 knew that his help, hope, and protection would always be found in the unfailing love and comfort of Christ. You can trust in that same life-changing truth today! Isn't Jesus wonderful?

Comfort-giver, soul-soother, You alone are
all I need today and all my days to come!

GREAT EXPECTATION

*The apostles performed many signs and wonders among
the people. . . . More and more men and women believed. . . .
People brought the sick into the streets and laid them. . .so that at
least Peter's shadow might fall on some of them as he passed by.*

ACTS 5:12, 14–15 NIV

The signs and wonders of the apostles were many. And though the Bible doesn't explain in detail what those "signs and wonders" were, we can assume they were the usual healings, casting out of demons, and other miracles. The fact that the apostles did these miracles in clear view of the people most definitely moved the minds and hearts of those watching. As unbelief turned to belief, more and more people joined the early church.

People had such faith in the healing miracles of Jesus that they took their sick friends and relatives and placed them so that even a part of Peter's *shadow* would fall on them when he passed by. While we know the power to heal didn't come from Peter's shadow—or even from Peter himself—this demonstrates a deep level of faith. They just *knew* healing would take place!

How about you? Do you have the kind of faith that comes free of doubt and full of great expectation? If you're struggling to wholeheartedly believe, talk to Jesus. He's listening.

*Lord, erase all doubt from my mind. Help me to
trust You fully—always expecting great things!*

SHATTERED FEAR

"Do not be afraid, Daughter Zion; see, your king is coming, seated on a donkey's colt." At first his disciples did not understand all this. Only after Jesus was glorified did they realize that these things had been written about him and that these things had been done to him.

JOHN 12:15–16 NIV

In a world where it seems as if power-hungry and egocentric people are running amok, it's a relief to turn to the Word of God for an attitude and outlook adjustment.

In the verses above, the Word is telling us not to be afraid—because we have a king who isn't out just to increase his wealth or power or crush our spirits. No. Our King, our Jesus, our Savior is humble. He's one who's neither militaristic nor materialistic. He comes to us in peace and humility. He doesn't pound on the doors of our hearts and minds, demanding entrance. He does just the opposite. He knocks, hoping we will open *our* doors. He makes His Word available, knowing that every day we delve into it, we come to another grand realization of who He actually is, what His Word actually means. And because of all these things, our fear is shattered. We are filled with calm, relief, and gratitude as the more we get to know and love Him, the more we reflect His glory and find our own selves becoming peace-loving, humble, and giving.

Help me, Jesus, become more like You!

GOD IS GOD!

Know this: GOD is God. . . . He made us; we didn't make him. We're his
people, his well-tended sheep. Enter with the password: "Thank you!"
Make yourselves at home, talking praise. Thank him. Worship him.
For GOD is sheer beauty, all-generous in love, loyal always and ever.

PSALM 100:3–5 MSG

"God is God." Is there any message more powerful, more beautiful, more hopeful than that?

We all struggle at times with our thoughts and emotions. Sometimes our minds swirl with negative thoughts. Our souls drown in doubt. Our courage is squashed by fearful feelings. Hope is elusive. We feel discouraged and lost, depressed and beaten down.

But if we follow Jesus, if we truly *know* Him, we can reach out to Him in faith and ask Him to soothe our troubled hearts. And He will come through. Why? Because God is God. He made us. He cares for us. He is beautiful, loving, and loyal—forever!

If you don't already know Him, start right now. Begin by reading these scriptures:

Romans 3:10, 23   Romans 10:9–10
Romans 6:23   Romans 10:13
Romans 5:8

If you do know Him, tell Him, "Thank You"! Praise Him for His generous love and loyalty.

God, thank You for all You are to me—my Creator, Savior, and friend.
No matter what's going on in the world or inside my heart, I can
rejoice, because You are who You are and You will never let me down.

YOUR DESIRED HAVEN

They. . .are at their wits' end [all their wisdom has come to nothing].
Then they cry to the Lord in their trouble, and He brings them out
of their distresses. He hushes the storm to a calm and to a gentle
whisper, so that the waves of the sea are still. Then the men are glad
because of the calm, and He brings them to their desired haven.
PSALM 107:27–30 AMPC

Seamen know of God's great power. For when they sail in great waters, they see sights few landlubbers will ever witness. Between sea creatures, endless horizon, eddies, and great winds and waves, they are witnesses to God's great works and wonders.

Yet when these same sailors are caught in a horrific storm, there are times when "their courage melts away because of their plight" (Psalm 107:26 AMPC). These seafarers know that all their wisdom cannot save them. They know there will be times when all they can do is cry out for God's help, praying He will bring them to safety.

Woman of the Way, be assured that God can hush your storms and calm your waves. Trust Him with all you are and have. Know that once you attain that heavenly peace amid earthly peril, you too will be glad as He brings you to your desired haven.

Lord, calmer of wind and waves, still my soul.
Bring me to my desired haven. Amen.

DESPERATE PRAYERS

LORD, hear my prayer! Listen to my plea! Don't turn away from me in my time of distress. Bend down to listen, and answer me quickly when I call to you.

PSALM 102:1–2 NLT

When was the last time you prayed a desperate prayer? You poured out your heart and soul. You ranted. You cried. You put it *all out there*—not so much the good, but definitely the bad and the ugly. You begged God to respond, not in His timing but *right now!*

Such is this prayer of the psalmist. His words are coming from a place of desperation. He is pleading with God to hear. . .to listen. And He isn't asking nicely: "Lord, would You mind listening to me today? If You have time, there are some things I'd like to share with You. Oh, You're busy? That's okay. Just get back to me later." Nope! This guy means business, and he doesn't hold back.

Sometimes life's situations make us desperate—for comfort. . .for healing. . .for a quick answer from our heavenly Father. And while it might be our practice to approach God quietly and calmly, the truth is He can handle the ranting, "I can't take it anymore!" prayers. He is a *big* God. Whatever you say to Him in prayer, He can handle it! He is faithful, and He is so, so good.

Faithful Father, I need You! Please comfort me, protect me, and give me Your peace.

FROM DESPAIR TO HOPE

*Nations will fear the name of the LORD, and all the
kings of the earth will fear your glory. For the LORD
builds up Zion; he appears in his glory.*

PSALM 102:15–16 ESV

This psalmist is under a lot of stress. He's in agony. (Read verses 1–12.) Yet, through the pouring out of his distressed heart and soul, something wonderful stirs in his spirit—a light begins to shine in the darkness. And, as he begins to think on the power and promises of the living God, his desperate words take a turn—from despair to hope.

There is comfort in knowing that God will make good on all He has promised. God is committed to building His church, and the psalmist has a heart for the same. This helps the psalmist hold on to hope and confidence, even in the middle of his personal trials.

Can you relate? Perhaps you're having a personal struggle of your very own. Maybe you're in utter agony. . .or maybe you're just a little stressed with the state of things. Either way, you could use some positivity in your life! What joy to know the same hope and comfort the psalmist experienced can also shine a light into your darkness. Take heart! Claim the power and promises of God as your very own!

*Heavenly Father, I am in distress! Please soothe my troubled soul.
I claim Your promises of hope, peace, comfort, and love today.*

ALWAYS IN REACH

Saul was still breathing out murderous threats against the Lord's disciples. He went to the high priest and asked him for letters to the synagogues in Damascus, so that if he found any there who belonged to the Way. . .he might take them as prisoners to Jerusalem. As he neared Damascus. . .a light from heaven flashed around him. He fell to the ground. . . . "Who are you, Lord?" Saul asked. "I am Jesus, whom you are persecuting," he replied. "Now get up and go into the city, and you will be told what you must do."

ACTS 9:1–6 NIV

Have you ever felt so far away from Jesus that you thought you were beyond saving? In our humanness, we've all fallen short—we're all sinners in need of redemption. We've cheated. We've lied. We've stolen. We've broken one—or more—of the Ten Commandments.

But how do your shortcomings stack up against Saul's? Saul had breathed "murderous threats against the Lord's disciples." Saul *hated* God's followers. He imprisoned and punished them. If anyone on earth was beyond saving, Saul would have been the guy.

And yet. . .God had a purpose for even someone like Saul. And on that road to Damascus, he had an encounter with Jesus that forever changed him.

Rest assured, your beautiful soul is never beyond saving. The Lord is waiting for you to take His hand. You are *always* within His reach.

Lord, I am never beyond Your saving grace. Thank You.

YOU BELONG

"Do what's right and do it in the right way, for salvation is just around the corner, my setting-things-right is about to go into action. How fortunate are you. . .who embrace them, who keep Sabbath and don't defile it, who watch your step and don't do anything evil! Make sure no outsider who now follows GOD ever has occasion to say, 'GOD put me in second-class. I don't really belong.' And make sure no physically mutilated person is ever made to think, 'I'm damaged goods. I don't really belong.'"
ISAIAH 56:1–3 MSG

Outcast. Unloved. Misfit. Damaged. "Less than. . ." We've probably identified with a few—if not all—of these descriptors at some point in our lives. Whether it's because of how we were raised or the by-product of years of negative self-talk, we've experienced the unwelcome feeling of being an outsider.

But God has a message for you, friend: *you belong!* When you stand for Him, strive to do what's right, and embrace your faith, He calls you *His.* And when you're His, He creates a brand-new identity for you. He calls you:

Loved (Zephaniah 3:17)   Blessed (Psalm 34:8)
Beautiful (Song of Solomon 4:7) Chosen (John 15:6)
Forgiven (Luke 7:48)

Embrace your identity in Christ. Know your worth. When He says, "you belong," He speaks truth!

*Heavenly Father, I am loved. I am beautiful. I am forgiven.
I am blessed. I am chosen. Because You say it, I believe it!*

FRAGRANCE

May my prayer be set before you like incense; may the lifting up of my hands be like the evening sacrifice.

PSALM 141:2 NIV

Have you ever wondered if your little prayers for help are irritating to God? Do you hesitate asking Him for directions in recovering lost keys or finding a parking spot? Don't. Because God actually loves it when you turn to Him for *anything*, big or small. He breathes in your prayers as fragrant incense. So you are never ever a bother to Him.

God looks at you with eyes of love. Every one of your prayers—long or short, frantic or calm—are a joy. He also gathers up and takes pleasure in all your "popcorn prayers"—little trusting thoughts that you send His way.

God is even more delighted when you offer Him your lifted hands, which is your way of expressing that He is your sovereign, almighty King and you are His loyal and loving servant.

So pray away today. And perhaps try worshiping God with your hands raised in adoration. It will lift your heart as well as His.

God, I trust that You hear even my smallest prayer and count it as special. Help me to remember to come to You with my big and small needs today. May my prayers, trusting thoughts, and upraised hands lift both our hearts today.

NEEDING MORE

*Show me now Your way, that I may know You [progressively
become more deeply and intimately acquainted with You, perceiving
and recognizing and understanding more strongly and clearly]
and that I may find favor in Your sight. . . . And the Lord said,
My Presence shall go with you, and I will give you rest.*

EXODUS 33:13–14 AMPC

God had said He would send an angel to go before Moses and His people (Exodus 33:2, 12–16). But Moses told God that His sending an angel was not enough. Moses wanted more. And so he asked for more. He asked for God's very presence to go with them. And God obliged.

Perhaps you too feel you need more. You want to know God better, to recognize Him, to understand His ways and means, to find out what He has in store for you and what His plans are.

Many of your questions can be answered by God's Word. Others can be addressed specifically to God in personal prayer.

Yet there is one thing that God wants you to be sure of, to take as fact. Just as with Moses, God's presence *is* walking with You. And He *will* give you all you need along the way—including His rest.

*I want to know You more dearly and see You more clearly, Lord.
Reveal Yourself to me. Walk with me and give me rest. Amen.*

WHAT WE DON'T DESERVE

It wasn't so long ago that you were mired in that old stagnant life of sin. You let the world. . .tell you how to live. . . . We all did it. . . . It's a wonder God didn't lose his temper and do away with the whole lot of us. Instead, immense in mercy and with an incredible love, he embraced us. He. . .made us alive in Christ.

EPHESIANS 2:1–4 MSG

We've all had "I deserve this" or "I deserve that" thoughts. We think we deserve *more* or *better* than we currently have. We want something someone else has. What we have isn't quite good enough. That's certainly the message of the world, isn't it?

And yet, we fail to acknowledge—or it fails to register—that we really don't "deserve" a single good thing. But, because of our sin, we *do* deserve to suffer the undesirable consequences.

But. . .God chose us. And in His choosing, He gifted us immense mercy, incredible love, life in Christ, and an eternal spot in our final, heavenly home.

Today, make it a priority to thank the heavenly Creator for choosing you. Thank Him for giving you everything you *don't* deserve. Thank Him for His love. Thank Him for Your best, blessed life.

Heavenly Creator, when You could have given me just what my sin-filled soul deserved, You—in Your abundant love— gave me everything I didn't. I am forever grateful.

YOUR BEST LIFE

*Keep my words and store up my commands. . . . Keep my
commands and you will live; guard my teachings as the
apple of your eye. Bind them on your fingers; write them
on the tablet of your heart. Say to wisdom, "You are
my sister," and to insight, "You are my relative."*

<small>PROVERBS 7:1–4 NIV</small>

Keep. Store up. Guard. Bind. Write. Say. Do *all* these things with God's
Word, and you will have life—*your best life*, that is. Because God's Word
is life, and we were created to live by it. When we become intimately
familiar with biblical truth, then we have a strong foundation for a truly
wonderful life.

When hard times come—*and they will*—a knowledge of God's hope
and healing will bring you through.

When temptations come—*and they will*—God's teachings will help
you stay on the path of faith and truth.

When enemies attack—*and they will*—God's promise of protection
and victory will shelter you.

What are you struggling with today, beautiful soul? Whatever it is,
trust God and His Word to carry you through it. His words will bring you
strength, comfort, and peace of mind. Open your Bible and see what He
has to say. Meditate on the message God has just for you.

Keep. Store up. Guard. Bind. Write. Say. Repeat!

*God, You are all good things. Help me to live my
best life with You and Your Word front and center!*

PRAY ALWAYS

Pray in the Spirit at all times and on every occasion. Stay alert and be persistent in your prayers for all believers. . . . And pray for me, too. Ask God to give me the right words so I can boldly explain God's mysterious plan that the Good News is for Jews and Gentiles alike. . . . Pray that I will keep on speaking boldly for him.

EPHESIANS 6:18–20 NLT

Communicating with God, and God communicating with us—both are so important in life! And prayer is how we accomplish our part of the equation. Through prayer, we can talk to God—thanking Him, asking for His help, expressing our needs, asking Him to help others.

Prayer shouldn't be a brief, one and done interaction. It should be an ongoing, daily conversation. This doesn't mean we stay home and do nothing but pray; but it does mean that we remain cognizant of the heavenly Father's presence in and around us all day long and that we stay in *regular* communication with Him. When you make this your daily practice, you'll find that even everyday thoughts turn into prayers. And you'll soon begin talking to God about *all* things—the big, the small, and everything in between. He hears—and He cares! Constant prayer . . .what a great way to grow your relationship with the heavenly Creator!

Father God, please help me make the practice of constant prayer a daily part of my life.

INFINITE VALUE

I once thought these things were valuable, but now I consider them worthless because. . .everything else is worthless when compared with the infinite value of knowing Christ Jesus my Lord. For his sake I have discarded everything else, counting it all as garbage, so that I could gain Christ and become one with him. I no longer count on my own righteousness through obeying the law; rather, I become righteous through faith in Christ.

<small>PHILIPPIANS 3:7–9 NLT</small>

There are so many things that we value—most of it "stuff," like our homes, vehicles, jewelry, techy gadgets. . .to name just a few.

When we place value on things according to the world's standards, we miss the mark when it comes to those things that have *eternal* value—what the writer of Philippians 3 calls "infinite value." Of all the things that matter, there's *one thing* more valuable than anything else in the world—it's knowing Jesus Christ as our Lord and Savior. In comparison, everything else is worthless garbage. All the stuff, our earthly possessions, don't matter one iota in the big picture of life.

What do you own that holds the most value to your heart and soul? Is it your relationship with Jesus? Have you gained Christ "and become one with him"?

My Savior, My Lord, compared to my relationship with You, everything else in life is worthless garbage. Help me keep my Christ-focus steady all the days of my life.

161

REMAIN IN HIS LOVE

"As the Father has loved me, so have I loved you. Now remain in my love. If you keep my commands, you will remain in my love, just as I have kept my Father's commands and remain in his love."

JOHN 15:9–10 NIV

Remaining in Christ's love is the only way to bear fruit that will last. John 15 gives us a beautiful picture of what bearing fruit means. What kind of fruit are we talking about here? The kind of fruit that makes a difference for Christ. The fruits of the Spirit are love, joy, peace, patience, kindness, goodness, faithfulness, gentleness, and self-control (Galatians 5:22–23). These are the fruits that honor God and come from a life that is growing in Him.

The Bible says that if we remain in God's love, we will bear much fruit. So how do we remain in His love? John 15:10 tells us the answer: "If you keep my commands, you will remain in my love." We can have complete joy and bear all kinds of spiritual fruit if we follow God's Word and live a life that pleases Him.

Just as a branch that has been cut off from the vine can do nothing, we can do nothing that matters if we aren't connected to the vine.

Father, help me stay connected to You so that I can bear the kind of fruit that matters. I know I can do nothing good without You. Amen.

POSITIVITY

We always thank God, the Father of our Lord Jesus Christ, when we pray for you, because we have heard of your faith in Christ Jesus and of the love you have for all God's people—the faith and love that spring from the hope stored up for you in heaven and about which you have already heard in the true message of the gospel that has come to you.

Colossians 1:3–6 niv

Here in Colossians, Paul is offering up a prayer of positivity—a prayer of thanks to God for the church at Colossae for their faith, their love, their hope.

When was the last time you prayed a prayer that was overflowing with thanks and appreciation for your fellow Christians? In our humanness, we tend to focus on the negative. Our prayers are filled with rants and requests that God change the people around us into what *we* would prefer them to be. Our prayers are typically quite selfish, aren't they?

God would surely rather have a conversation with us about the gifts and good qualities we see in others. And all the good is where our heart *should* take notice. Because, if we look for the good, that is exactly what we will find! Ask God to help you look for the positive today—and He surely will!

Please give me Your eyes to see the good in others,
Lord Jesus. I want to paint the words of my prayers
with positivity, gratefulness, and grace.

THE SAME CLAY

So I went to the potter's house, and. . .the potter was there,
working away at his wheel. Whenever the pot the potter
was working on turned out badly, as sometimes happens
when you are working with clay, the potter would simply
start over and use the same clay to make another pot.
JEREMIAH 18:3–4 MSG

The potter is bent over his wheel, working to create a flawless master-piece. He stops for a minute, takes a critical look at the finished product, and decides it's inadequate. Perhaps the pot is blemished in some way; maybe it isn't shaped quite right for its intended purpose. Either way, the potter decides to start over. But take notice: he doesn't begin his new project with new clay. No! He starts over, using the *very same clay* from the original, imperfect pot.

Just like the potter, God often starts over with us—using the same "clay." He doesn't cast us aside and put someone else, *someone better*, in our place. He uses us, just as we are, and keeps working until He is satisfied—no matter how long it takes. And in His working, His shaping and crafting, He smooths away our imperfections—our stubbornness, our impatience, our selfish streaks—and keeps refining us in the process. God created us for His good purpose, and He won't ever stop molding us into the beautiful women He intends us to be. Praise Him!

Heavenly potter, thank You for working on me and in me.

THE LORD IS MY SHEPHERD

"I myself will gather the remnant of my flock out of all the countries where I have driven them and will bring them back to their pasture, where they will be fruitful and increase in number. I will place shepherds over them who will tend them, and they will no longer be afraid or terrified, nor will any be missing," declares the Lord.

JEREMIAH 23:3–4 NIV

The picture of white, woolly sheep peacefully dotting a verdant hillside is like a postcard come to life. It's hard to imagine these gentle animals ever being terrified in such a scene. But should a predator creep close to the flock, the animals would begin to bleat nervously.

Sheep aren't the smartest creatures. If they're grazing far away from their pen, they won't find their own way home. They need a shepherd to guide them. Without that leader, they'll become even more scattered and fearful, and the weakest ones will be a target for a clever coyote.

We aren't so different from the sheep (though hopefully slightly smarter).

When we walk far from the security God offers, we have a hard time finding the way home. We need someone to protect us from our own folly, to calm us when we're under attack from evil forces of the enemy, and to firmly guide us to gather close together, support each other, and run back to safety.

God, I'm glad I can count on You to bring me home. Amen.

WHO ARE YOU, REALLY?

*Put on then, as God's chosen ones, holy and beloved,
compassionate hearts, kindness, humility, meekness,
and patience, bearing with one another and, if one has
a complaint against another, forgiving each other; as the
Lord has forgiven you. . . . And above all these put on love,
which binds everything together in perfect harmony. And let
the peace of Christ rule in your hearts. . . . And be thankful.*

COLOSSIANS 3:12–15 ESV

"Who are you?" It's a common question, but have you ever really, truly thought about who you are? It isn't as simple as your name; it's not where you come from; not what you do for a living; and not who your parents, brothers, sisters, cousins, friends are. It's something much, much deeper than that.

Who you are involves your character—it's what's in your heart. And when you choose to follow Christ, your faith and your pursuit of Him are what make you who you are. Your life in Him is the most important thing about you, dear one! Because when you say *yes* to His invitation, you become a brand-new person, a child of God! And others will know you by what's in your heart!

*Lord Jesus, when others look at me, do they see a heart that beats
with love, compassion, wisdom, gratitude, grace, forgiveness,
kindness, peace, and patience? I want others to see You in me!*

WITHOUT A WORD

*Everywhere the report has gone forth of your faith in God
[of your leaning of your whole personality on Him in complete
trust and confidence in His power, wisdom, and goodness]. So we
[find that we] never need to tell people anything [further about it].*

1 THESSALONIANS 1:8 AMPC

These men of God "oozed" their faith wherever they went! It was evident in their character, their trust and confidence, their wisdom and goodness.

Imagine being so sold out for God that every person you met took notice.

Everywhere you went—in your neighborhood, at work, running errands—people could see the light of Christ shining through because of your "vibe." You radiated kindness and love, care and compassion, wisdom and peace. You were noticeably different from the rest of the world.

Wouldn't that be something if you went about your everyday life and never had to bring up the subject of the Christian faith because people noticed something different—something *special*—about you? And they just had to know what it was?

Purpose to be the kind of woman who radiates Christ. When you show others who He is in your actions and character, they will begin to ask questions, and doors will open to share Jesus with the world!

*Father God, thank You for showing me that I don't always need
to shout "Jesus!" from the rooftops. I can quietly share You
with the world through the woman You created me to be.*

BLOOM AND GROW

"Their lives will be like a well-watered garden, never again left to dry up. Young women will dance and be happy, young men and old men will join in. I'll convert their weeping into laughter."

JEREMIAH 31:12–13 MSG

Imagine a dead, withered flower garden. Brown leaves rustle and scatter in the breeze; full, colorful blooms have faded; a once-lovely floral aroma has been overtaken by the smell of death and decay. This sad, lifeless flower garden bears resemblance to our lives without Christ. Without Him, we have no sunshine, no rain, no pruning—no life! When He's missing, our story is devoid of hope and light.

But *with* Him? When Christ is front and center in our lives, we are like a well-cared-for garden. Lush and bursting with color. . .an aroma, sweet and pleasant! We get just enough sunshine, the perfect amount of rain (right down to the last drop!). Our petals stretch out, colorful and full. And Christ continues to work, day by day, pruning and caring for us so that we can bloom and grow into the splendid daughters He meant for us to be.

On days when you feel dried up and hopeless, reach out to the master gardener. Allow Him to pluck, prune, and drench your parched soul in His love and compassion. He will bring what's dead to life again.

Master gardener, I invite you to work on the dried-up parts of my soul. Please give me light, hope, and life!

YOU CAN DO IT!

Rejoice always, pray continually, give thanks in all circumstances; for this is God's will for you.
1 THESSALONIANS 5:16–18 NIV

Worship is how we honor God. These verses from 1 Thessalonians give good advice for our personal worship:

1. Rejoice always. Not only should we feel our joy, but others should be able to *see* it. We can rejoice all the time because our joy isn't dependent on our ever-changing circumstances, but it *is* dependent on our unchanging God!

2. Pray always. While this doesn't mean we're always on our knees, hands folded, eyes closed, it *does* mean that we stay in constant conversation with God. This is an every-minute-of-the-day kind of interaction with Him. It doesn't matter whether you pray aloud or in silence, standing or on your knees, at work or at home, day or night. You are *never* in a place where you can't pray.

3. Give thanks, no matter what. While you won't be thankful *for* every circumstance that comes your way, you can be thankful *in* every circumstance. This is because our loving heavenly Creator has everything under control—nothing is left to chance.

If you read these guidelines and are thinking it seems impossible, know that with God's help, you *can* do it!

Lord, I need Your help today to be joyful, pray, and give thanks—always and in all circumstances.

GOD OF RESTORATION

"I will surely gather them from all the lands where I banish them in my. . .great wrath; I will bring them back. . . . They will be my people, and I will be their God. . . . I will make an everlasting covenant with them. . . . I will rejoice in doing them good and will assuredly plant them in this land with all my heart and soul."

JEREMIAH 32:37–38, 40–41 NIV

When we fall short of God's expectations, we experience feelings of shame and regret. Sometimes we get stuck in those feelings. Surely, God is *still* mad at us. He will *never* forgive us. And, in the middle of our mess, we often feel like the worst humanity has to offer.

And yet our God of judgment is also a God of restoration. He promises *both*—one is as sure as the other! As these verses from Jeremiah 32 remind us, those who had been banished, He *will* gather them back together again. He *will* be their God; and they will belong to Him—along with future generations. He *will* bless them and do good to them. He *will* inspire them so they never turn away from Him. And He makes good on these promises!

If you're struggling today, take heart! Invite the God of restoration to draw you back to Him. He will, with all His heart and soul!

Father, thank You for always bringing me back to You.

NEVER FORSAKEN

O God, You have taught me from my youth; and to this day I declare Your wondrous works. Now also when I am old and grayheaded, O God, do not forsake me, until I declare Your strength to this generation, Your power to everyone who is to come.

PSALM 71:17–18 NKJV

Have you ever known the pain of betrayal? Ever been badly hurt by someone who promised to stick by you, no matter what? Losing a friend can be gut-wrenching. No one enters a relationship hoping to be abandoned. This sort of heartache can linger and cause issues years after the fact.

No matter how badly broken your heart has been in the past, you can experience healing and wholeness again. Give that broken heart to the Lord and watch Him miraculously ease your pain. Best of all, He will stick close to you. In fact, He promises to never leave you. No rejection. No betrayal. No abandonment. When you enter a relationship with the Lord, it's for eternity. Now, that's a friendship worth having!

You've always stuck with me, Lord, even when I didn't deserve it. From the day I drew my first breath on planet Earth until this very moment, You've been right there, gently guiding me and giving me strength to overcome every obstacle. You've never left my side, Father, and You never will. I can trust in You, Lord. Amen.

IN THE "DOWN" SEASONS

*Pray that we'll be rescued from these troublemakers who
are trying to do us in. . . . The Master never lets us down.
He'll stick by you and protect you from evil.*

2 THESSALONIANS 3:2–3 MSG

Our lives are full of ups, downs, and in-betweens. And there seem to be seasons that weigh heavily upon us, with one "down" after another . . .and no relief in sight. During those times, we often struggle to keep hold of our faith. We think, *Where is God? I need His rescue. I need His strength. And He doesn't seem to be hearing my cries for help. Doesn't He care?*

If we'd only take the time to notice, these difficult seasons are often when we can see and feel God the most. We just need to shift our focus from *us* to *Him.* When we do that, we experience a perspective transformation—and we can clearly see His hand in our lives. Caring. Providing. Protecting. Loving.

As Paul noted in 2 Thessalonians 3, "The Master never lets us down." When things were difficult for Paul and his fellow Christ-followers, they trusted God. They knew He would take care of things—and His people. It was true then, and the same is true for us today!

*Lord Jesus, help me to shift my focus from me
to You. Thank You for always being here,
loving me, and caring for me in my "down" seasons.
I trust You have everything under control.*

READY FOR CHANGE

*"If my people, who are called by my name, will humble
themselves and pray and seek my face and turn from
their wicked ways, then I will hear from heaven, and I
will forgive their sin and will heal their land."*

2 CHRONICLES 7:14 NIV

How we yearn for the "good old days." Many of us remember our child-hood years with nostalgia about a kinder, gentler time. We think that things were much better then. King Solomon might have thought the same thing when this verse was given to him at the dedication of the temple. The verse is a call for revival.

Revival doesn't have to be a corporate event. Sometimes, it needs to be personal. The statement is conditional: if we will meet the requirements on our end, we can be sure that God will move on His end.

*Sovereign God, I come to You wanting revival in my life. I humble
myself before You, understanding that I cannot do anything without
You. Please rekindle my desire for You and hear my pledge to erase
anything from my life that does not please You. I know that You
will hear me; help me and heal me as You have promised. Amen!*

A DIFFERENT PLAN

Jesus Christ came into the world to save sinners. I'm proof—
Public Sinner Number One—of someone who could
never have made it apart from sheer mercy. And now he
shows me off—evidence of his endless patience—to those
who are right on the edge of trusting him forever.
1 TIMOTHY 1:15–16 MSG

Saul was the chief of all sinners—the very worst! Blasphemer. Persecutor. Dangerous. Corrupt. He relished the punishment of Christ-followers. Christ-followers literally quaked in their sandals at the mere whisper of Saul's name.

And yet. . .he, *Saul*, was chosen. This worst-among-all-sinners was hand-picked by the heavenly Father to share the gospel message. (Read the full story in Acts 9.) Surely, Saul had been deemed "hopeless" and "forever lost" among the Christian community of his day. But God had a different plan. And on the road to Damascus, Saul's heart began to beat for Jesus. Along with his heart-change, God gave him a name change too. Saul became Paul—a man on fire for Jesus. If anyone ever doubted God could use even the worst of sinners, Paul was proof to the contrary.

Take Paul's story to heart today. Remember you can *always* count on this: Jesus came into the world to save sinners—and there's living proof in the lives of the people He has transformed!

Precious Savior, I am so thankful that no one is ever beyond
Your reach. May my life be proof of Your wonderful promise!

MIXED MESSAGES

You've been raised on the Message of the faith and have followed sound teaching. Now pass on this counsel to the followers of Jesus there, and you'll be a good servant of Jesus. Stay clear of silly stories that get dressed up as religion. Exercise daily in God. . . . Workouts in the gymnasium are useful, but a disciplined life in God is far more so. . . . Take it to heart.

1 TIMOTHY 4:6–9 MSG

There are so many mixed messages about God, salvation, creation, heaven, and eternity—really, about any topic related to religion and spirituality. Every day, someone new is claiming to be an expert on faith and religion. It's impossible to keep up with the book releases, podcasts, social media posts. And it can get a little confusing.

While some messages ring true, others are obviously *way* off base. And those messages are easy to dismiss. But there are messages sprinkled with *a touch of truth*; and even though they're nothing more than silly stories tied up with a pretty bow, they draw you in. Before any confusion sets in, we need to weigh these messages against the trusted authority of God's Word. It will *always* tell you the truth. It will *never* lead you astray. It will show you the way today—and all your days to come.

Heavenly Father, no silly stories wrapped in pretty packages for me! Thank You for the truth of Your Word!

LAUNCHING OUT

Jesus said. . .It is I; be not afraid! [I Am; stop being frightened!]
Then they were quite willing and glad for Him to come into the boat.
And now the boat went at once to the land they had steered toward.
JOHN 6:20–21 AMPC

We're ready to launch out on a new venture. We wait for Jesus, but He seems delayed. So we decide to set sail in darkness. Unable to see what lies fore or aft, fear begins to creep in. We begin looking furtively around, wondering what threat may be approaching. Suddenly the wind rises and our boat rocks from unforeseen waves. We begin to lose our bearings, frantically trying to guide our little craft, the oars held tight in our white-knuckled grip as we roll with every dip and crest of the waves. The cold seawater ripping across our faces, we begin to doubt our vision. Feeling as if we're making no progress at all, discouragement adds to our fears and loss of direction.

Then a ghostly figure approaches our craft. We scream in surprise but then hear a soothing voice: "It's only Me! Don't be afraid!" Deliriously relieved, we let Jesus into our boat. The next thing you know, we arrive at the destination for which we'd been striving.

When trouble arises, trust that Christ sees your struggle and is on His way. Your job? To let Him into your boat.

Thank You, Lord, for helping me reach the shore to which I'm heading!

CERTAIN THINGS

Teach those who are rich. . .not to trust in their money. . . .
Their trust should be in God. . . . Tell them to use their money to do
good. . . . By doing this they will be storing up their treasure as a
good foundation for the future so that they may experience true life.
1 TIMOTHY 6:17–19 NLT

If you've ever had money—or experienced the lack thereof—you know that one thing is certain: it's 100 percent unreliable. Money can be here in an instant and gone the next—especially in an unpredictable world of inflation, unexpected bills, and ever-increasing taxes. Money often disappears as fast as—or faster than!—you can make it.

Our trust would be better served if we placed it in the reliability of God and His beautiful promise of heaven. When we focus our priorities as God would have us do, then our money becomes a tool to be used to further His kingdom rather than a crutch that feeds our greed. When we use our money for good, only then do we begin to truly experience the life God intended: a life rich in blessings and treasures that can't be bought.

Father God, so many things in this life are uncertain. I am so
glad I can fully depend on You. Help me to get—and keep!—
my priorities straight. I want to experience a life rich in blessings.

GRATITUDE OVER GRUMBLING

Every time I say your name in prayer—which is practically all the time—I thank God for you, the God I worship with my whole life in the tradition of my ancestors. I miss you a lot, especially when I remember that last tearful good-bye, and I look forward to a joy-packed reunion.

2 TIMOTHY 1:3–4 MSG

These verses are oozing with gratitude and hope. And while it's not uncommon to come across the thoughts and prayers of a thankful heart in the scriptures, what is most extraordinary in this instance is that Paul—the writer of these words—was in prison for sharing the gospel message. The ancient prison where he was held captive was likely dark, damp, dirty, cold, and lonely. . .certainly not an environment conducive to "all the feels."

Yet, in this uncomfortable, unfair, unfortunate situation, Paul clung to joy and hope. He continued to pray and worship. What a wonderful example when we struggle with situations and circumstances beyond our control. Because, like Paul, we too can depend on the master Creator to give us strength in our weakness, comfort in our pain, joy in our suffering. When we keep an attitude of gratitude front and center in our lives, joy is sure to follow.

When it feels like the world is crashing down, grab God's hand and hold tight. He won't let go!

Giver of hope, comfort, and strength, infuse my heart with Your power. Today, I choose gratitude over grumbling.

GO WITH THE GLOW

*The Israelites set out whenever the cloud was taken up from the tabernacle throughout all the stages of their journey. If the cloud was not taken up, they did not set out until the day it was taken up. For the cloud of the L*ORD *was over the tabernacle by day, and there was a fire inside the cloud by night, visible to the entire house of Israel throughout all the stages of their journey.*
EXODUS 40:36–38 HCSB

When you are not sure where to go, when to go, or how long to rest, look to the only guide you will ever need: God. That's what the Israelites did.

The cloud was the token of God's presence. His people could see it in the daytime hours, hovering over the tabernacle. At night, the Israelites could see the fire aglow within the cloud. And these symbols, these embodiments of God's presence, could be seen by everyone! The entire house of Israel. . .every single step and stage of its journey.

You too have a token of God's presence. You have the Holy Spirit who teaches you how to follow the ways of Jesus. It's that burning presence deep within you. Where and when it leads, you are to go. Where and when it doesn't go, you are to rest.

*What a relief, Lord, knowing all I have to do is follow
the glow of the Spirit and all will be well. Amen!*

A Strong Foundation

*Everyone who hears these words of Mine and acts upon them
[obeying them] will be like a sensible. . .man who built his house upon
the rock. And the rain fell and the floods came and the winds blew and
beat against that house; yet it did not fall, because it had been founded
on the rock. And everyone who hears these words of Mine and does
not do them will be like a stupid. . .man who built his house upon the
sand. And the rain fell and the floods came and the winds blew and beat
against that house, and it fell—and great and complete was the fall of it.*
MATTHEW 7:24–27 AMPC

Obedience seems like such a stiff, serious, *b-o-r-i-n-g* subject, doesn't it?
If you "obey," aren't you really giving up your own will. . .your own
desires. . .to instead follow the path someone else—in this case, God—
has set for you? And can that really lead to a fulfilling life?

These words of Jesus in Matthew 7 confirm that the answer is
yes—obedience to God *always* leads to a better life, creating a strong,
faith-filled foundation to help you stand firm when the storms of life
blow and batter against your weary soul. Allow your faithful obedience
to transform your life—willingly give up your *imperfect* will for His *perfect*
plan. Your house will stand strong!

Father God, help me build my house upon the rock!

FLAWLESS!

As for God, his way is perfect: The LORD's word is flawless;
he shields all who take refuge in him. For who is God besides
the LORD? And who is the Rock except our God? It is God
who arms me with strength and keeps my way secure.

PSALM 18:30–32 NIV

Dictionary.com defines the word *flawless* as: "having no defects or faults, especially none that diminish the value of something" and "having no discernible blemishes or shortcomings; perfect." Can you name anyone or anything that fits these descriptions? Maybe a lovely red rose in full bloom. Your best friend, who is a stunning beauty. The fragrance of fresh-brewed coffee first thing in the morning. The smell of salty air floating on the warm ocean breeze.

While there are many things in life that bring us sheer delight because of their wonderful qualities, the truth is none of those things is truly perfect or flawless. *But* you do know someone who is the very definition of flawless Himself. . .the Lord and Savior, Jesus Christ. And He alone offers just what you need—security, strength, protection, comfort, and more! He is your shield and your rock. He sets you on the right path with His flawless Word and ways.

Praise Him for drawing your heart near to His. . .for being the perfection you need today and all your days to come.

My Redeemer, I thank You for Your flawless
ways. . .for Your perfect Word that guides my life!

GOD'S PERFECT LAWS

The law of the LORD is perfect, refreshing the soul. The statutes of the LORD are trustworthy, making wise the simple. The precepts of the LORD are right, giving joy to the heart. The commands of the LORD are radiant, giving light to the eyes. The fear of the LORD is pure, enduring forever. The decrees of the LORD are firm, and all of them are righteous.

PSALM 19:7–9 NIV

Laws are created for the good of all people. They are meant to keep us safe, protect our rights, and more. Speed limits are put in place to keep the roads safer for traveling. And we have laws that guarantee basic human freedoms—freedom of speech, religion, and the press.

But no matter how good man-made laws are, they fall short—which is why many laws are often amended over time. In contrast, the laws of our heavenly Father are "perfect, "trustworthy," and they stand firm forever. His commands are righteous because they stem from His goodness and love.

The bottom line? God is good. And obeying His laws and commands will *always* lead to good things as well. If you're in need of a soul refreshing today, ask Him to give you His wisdom and to lead you all your days. Commit to obeying His laws, and your heart will be filled with joy!

Heavenly Father, thank You for Your perfect, enduring laws. You are so, so good, and I love You!

WHO GOD HEARS

The LORD is far from the wicked,
but he hears the prayers of the righteous.
PROVERBS 15:29 NLT

One of the countless, wonderful things about God is that He's a gentleman. As powerful as He is, He rarely pushes in where He's not wanted, except in cases where justice demands it.

God remains far from the wicked, for the wicked push Him away. They don't want Him around. They make choices against the Almighty and disregard His ways. Then, when they land themselves in trouble with no way out, help is nowhere to be found. They choose to exclude the one who could help them. In the end, they have no one.

But when the righteous call His name, He hears. Though none of us is righteous on our own, we can claim righteousness through Jesus Christ. He alone is righteous, and He covers us like a cloak. When we call on God, He sees the righteousness that covers us through Christ and recognizes us as His children. He leans over and listens carefully to our words because we belong to Him. He loves us.

Next time it seems like God isn't listening, perhaps we should examine our hearts. Have we pushed God away? Have we accepted the price His Son, Jesus Christ, paid on our behalf? If not, we can't claim righteousness. If we have, we can trust that He's never far away. He hears us.

Dear Father, thank You for making me
righteous through Your Son, Jesus. Amen.

FREE AT LAST

Along about midnight, Paul and Silas were at prayer and singing a robust hymn to God. The other prisoners couldn't believe their ears. Then, without warning, a huge earthquake! The jailhouse tottered, every door flew open, all the prisoners were loose.
ACTS 16:25–26 MSG

Chances are you've experienced hurt of some kind or another. Sometimes the scars and debilitating wounds are visible, but often they remain hidden deep inside, shared only with the few you think you can trust, or perhaps no one at all.

Paul and Silas were beaten and unjustly thrown into jail, simply for sharing their faith. In Acts 16:16–40, they found themselves imprisoned with bruises and pain, no doubt on the inside as well as the outside. While they praised God through their suffering and heartbreak, God delivered them from their chains. He set them free, literally. In a difficult place, Paul and Silas chose to praise God anyway.

God's deliverance can happen rapidly or it can take some time. Either way, God will set you free from the pain. While you're waiting, praise God. Doing so can comfort your heart and soothe the broken places in your life. Praise can give you the strength you need to let go, forgive, and break out of the chains.

Lord, I'm in one of those difficult places now. I open my heart and my mouth in praise to You today. I trust You to set me free from the pain.

LEAN BACK

Be still and rest in the Lord; wait for Him and patiently lean yourself upon Him; fret not yourself because of him who prospers in his way, because of the man who brings wicked devices to pass. Cease from anger and forsake wrath; fret not yourself—it tends only to evildoing. For evildoers shall be cut off, but those who wait and hope and look for the Lord. . .shall inherit the earth.

PSALM 37:7–9 AMPC

When someone wants to pick a fight, it's hard to stand still, to not get angry. All those instincts that prompt you to strike back at the one who has struck you are just what God wants you to ignore. Getting angry and fighting back only make things worse.

Instead of lifting a hand to harm the one who has harmed you, you're to lean back against God, to be still, to rest in the one who wants you to be a woman of peace—not turmoil. Why? Because it's peaceful women of strength, character, and faith who will inherit the earth.

Remember, God will take care of the evildoers. He'll cut them off at the knees. Meanwhile, *your* steps and plans will be directed by the Lord. Walk in time with Him and you'll never lose your way.

Thank You, Lord, for being my guard, guide, refuge, and stronghold. Help me to leave the wicked in Your hands so that I can keep my peace and joy in You. Amen.

CARE AND KEEPING

The earth is the LORD's and the fullness thereof,
the world and those who dwell therein, for he has founded
it upon the seas and established it upon the rivers.

PSALM 24:1–2 ESV

When you think about the things you own—your home, your car, your collectibles—how does it make you feel? Do you hold tightly to those things? Do you work hard to keep them clean and in good condition? Have you taken steps to keep them safe from harm and destruction? Do they give you a sense of pride?

Now think about our world and its ownership. Did you know that God has 100 percent ownership of the earth and everything in it? After all, He made earth. . .He formed it. . .He filled it with life. He is ruler over all! And everything on this planet has been lent to you and to me. And we are charged with the care and keeping of it.

If you take such amazing care of your own possessions, what better care should you give to the heavenly Creator's workmanship? Today think about some things you might want to change in the ways you live, work, and play on this planet. Then ask God to help you follow through in your actions.

Lord Jesus, I thank You for your creation. I want to
take utmost care of the things You've entrusted to me.
And help me be a good example to others.

THE FAITH PERFECTER

And Jesus rebuked the demon, and it came out of him, and the boy was healed instantly. Then the disciples came to Jesus privately and said, "Why could we not cast it out?" He said to them, "Because of your little faith. For truly, I say to you, if you have faith like a grain of mustard seed, you will say to this mountain, 'Move from here to there,' and it will move, and nothing will be impossible for you."

MATTHEW 17:18–21 ESV

If you've been a Christian for long, you're quite familiar with Jesus' parable of the mustard seed. And while you may know that a mustard seed is quite tiny, you may not know that the length of a mustard seed can be as little as 1 millimeter! And Jesus used this *minuscule* seed to make a *very big* point in His story.

His disciples asked Jesus why they were unable to cast out the demon themselves. Without hesitation, Jesus replied that they didn't have enough faith. . .*but* with a mustard-seed-sized faith, they could move mountains! In fact, He even added, "*Nothing* will be impossible for you" (emphasis added).

What is the size of your faith? Are you moving mountains, sister? Or does your faith need some growing? Either way, talk to the one who holds the world in the palm of His hands—He's the "author and perfecter" of your faith (Hebrews 12:2).

Father God, help me to move mountains!

IN ALL SEASONS, PRAY!

Is anyone among you in trouble? Let them pray. Is anyone happy?
Let them sing songs of praise. Is anyone among you sick? Let them
call the elders of the church to pray over them. . . . And the prayer
offered in faith will make the sick person well; the Lord will raise
them up. If they have sinned, they will be forgiven. Therefore confess
your sins to each other and pray for each other so that you may be
healed. The prayer of a righteous person is powerful and effective.

JAMES 5:13–16 NIV

In life, we experience seasons—some easy, others difficult; some joyful, others sad; some courageous, others fearful; some comfortable, others quite miserable. Life's unique seasons evoke reactions that run the gamut—laughter, tears, humility, grit, persistence, resilience—no two seasons are the same. But there is always one reaction that is appropriate for all seasons, and that is prayer!

Scripture tells us if we're in trouble, we should pray. We should also pray when we're experiencing illness or joy, struggling with sin and temptation. *Whatever* it is, there's never a time when we shouldn't pray, because prayer brings comfort, healing, calm, and restoration to our souls. Truly, there's *nothing* that time with Jesus can't fix.

See for yourself. Whatever season you're in, tell God all about it. Then quiet your heart and listen.

Heavenly Father, thank You for the gift of prayer.
I trust You'll listen in every season of my life.

SCRIPTURE INDEX

OLD TESTAMENT

NEW TESTAMENT